The Historical Basis of Welsh Nationalism

A Series of lectures

by

A. W. WADE-EVANS
T. JONES PIERCE
CEINWEN THOMAS
A. O. H. JARMAN
D. GWENALLT JONES
GWYNFOR EVANS

CONTENTS.

FOREWORD	i.
PROLEGOMENA TO A STUDY OF EARLY WELSH HISTORY	1
THE AGE OF THE PRINCES	42
FROM THE FALL OF LLYWELYN TO THE TUDOR PERIOD	60
WALES A PART OF ENGLAND, 1485—1800	79
NATIONAL MOVEMENTS IN WALES IN THE NINETEENTH CENTURY	99
THE TWENTIETH CENTURY AND PLAID CYMRU	130

FOREWORD.

THE late Prosser Rhys, in his noble poem on Wales, in which he expresses the very essence of Welsh Nationalism, appeals to our nation to come to terms, or to enter into a covenant, a reconciliation, with her splendid past. No words could better express the motive of the executive committee of Plaid Cymru in inviting six Welsh scholars to address the party's annual summer school at Abergavenny in 1946. Their lectures on that occasion form the contents of this book, except that some of them have undergone revision by their authors, and that the opening lecture has been considerably augmented in order to fill the long gap between the beginnings of the nation as therein described and the period of the second lecture.

Members of our party are often reminded that no nation can live on its past, but this is no more than a dangerous half-truth, as it is equally certain that no nation can know the direction of its true development without the knowledge of its origins and the lines of its growth. We believe with Patrick Pearse that the ideal of all healthy politics should be to make the present a rational continuation of the past, and we do not look on our own history as if it were a cave to shelter the irresolute dreamer from the storms of his own day, but rather as a power-house that will give him the strength to withstand them.

No attempt has been made in these lectures to present every aspect of Welsh history, but to re-examine that history, as we know it to-day, for the evidence it has to offer of an awareness among the people of Wales, from period to period, of their own distinctiveness as a people, and to discuss the institutions and movements among them which have upheld this awareness. Not one of the lecturers would claim to have exhausted his subject, nor within the scope of a single lecture to have done more than to introduce it. Not one of them was expected to follow a political "party-line", but rather to be guided solely by his own insight. They are not all members, even, of the Party which is sponsoring the work, and we shall be both surprised and disappointed if many of the statements made in this book will not provoke keen discussion both within and outside the ranks of Plaid Cymru. Keen argument is to be welcomed for we know that heat and light are closely related.

If this book should create a livelier curiosity in our readers, and thus inspire them to greater efforts to know the rock whence they are hewn, it will have achieved much of its purpose. There are many aspects to the relationship between nationalism and history, but it cannot be denied that love of country has been among the main incentives to the study of a nation's past, and it is our conviction that that love is a worthy sentiment.

Three of these lectures were delivered in English, namely the first, the third and the last. The lecturers themselves translated the second and the fourth from Welsh, and the editor is responsible for the English of the fifth. The editor also wishes to extend his personal thanks, and the thanks of the executive committee of Plaid Cymru, to all who have helped in the preparation of this book.

D. M. L.

PROLEGOMENA TO A STUDY OF EARLY WELSH HISTORY.

I HAVE been asked to speak to you to-day as an authority on Welsh history. Let me at once disclaim any and every pretension to be an authority. I am now, as I have always been, a lone inquirer into the subject. And I hope that you will hear me this afternoon as one speaking in that spirit, even if I may seem at times to be speaking somewhat dogmatically.

The question as to when Welsh national life begins is an important c .e for our nation. The general uncertainty about it in the mind of modern Wales is a tragedy. Yet the Welsh have always felt the need of knowing whence they came. Long before the Normans arrived, the Britons of Wales had traced their honourable descent from Brutus, a Roman consul; also, from Britto, a descendant of Aeneas of Troy.[1] As much as to say that the Britons were of the same high origin as the Romans, the Britons being, as one very early document puts it, *filii Romanorum*, sons of the Romans, of the stock of Troy.[2] And the Welsh clung to that faith as long as it was possible to cling to it. Symbolically of course it was true. For why? The people of Wales as a people had never known themselves to be such, until they tumbled to it in their Roman surroundings. They were already Romans before they realized that they were Britons. They had never called themselves Britons, nor could they have done so, till Roman times, for the very word Britons is only a derivative of *Britanni*, the inhabitants of Britannia, and, as some maintain,[3] no one called this island Britannia, till Julius Cæsar set the fashion.

Then centuries elapsed, a thousand years, and the symbol of Brutus, the Roman consul, faded out. Rome, and the Roman empire, in which the Britons of Wales had first found themselves, receded in their imaginations, until at length in the minds of the bewildered people Rome stood not for that famous empire whence they had sprung, but for the Papacy, the Church Catholic, nicknamed Popery and worse. Thereupon the Cymry began to look round for some other honourable pedigree in order to maintain the dignity of the nation, so anxious were they about their origins. And they found it just where they would like to find it, *i.e.*, in the Welsh Protestant Bible. There it was in black and white, in the inspired writings, for (as they were told) anyone with half an eye could see that Cymro, Welshman, was only Gomero, and that the Cymry were plainly the descendants of Gomer, the son of Japheth, the son of Noah. It must have come to them like a message from heaven.

---

1. Nennius's " History of the Britons " (ed. by A. W. Wade-Evans) S.P.C.K., 1938 7, 11.
2. *Chronica Minora* (ed. T. Mommsen, 1894), 149 n 1; *Arch. Camb.* (1937), 66, 76.
3. Gweirydd ap Rhys, *Hanes y Brytaniaid a'r Cymry*, i, 12.

But consider the price, which the Welsh of the nineteenth century had to pay for substituting Gomer the son of Japheth for Brutus, the Roman consul, and for Britto of the lineage of Troy—verily a lesson to us for all time to be careful of our symbols. For by that substitution the Cymry lost all sense of their historic origin from the Britons of Roman times, and of their age-long association with the Roman empire and with western civilization in general. And this fateful detachment of the Welsh from the main current of the civilized west swept them more completely than ever into the sidestreams of London and Canterbury. Cut off from the Roman west, cut off even from Ireland, the Cymry in their isolation would have been swallowed up and lost in the story of Hengist and Horsa, were it not that in their disillusionment they began as it were to grope and fumble for the rock whence they were hewn.

It is indeed a salutary saying that if you want to go forward, you must always go back. There will be no true resurrection of Wales, till Wales recovers the truth of her origins. 'Nothing can reinvigorate itself or snatch itself from decay save by a return upon itself and a recapture of its own past.' So now, when Brutus, the Roman consul, has served his purpose, and the Star of Gomer, the son of Japheth, has sunk below the horizon, it must needs be that the Welsh mind, awakening out of slumber and fanciful dreams, should seek diligently for some more substantial figure and symbol, wherewith to give the Welsh nation once again an honourable start.

Unless I am mistaken, I believe that the average idea of Welsh origins may be stated simply as follows. The Ancient Britons occupied the whole island of Britain. They were conquered by the Romans. The Romans departed. Then the Saxons landed and expelled the Ancient Britons out of England into Wales. 'Glen after glen and mountain after mountain slipped from the grasp of the old inhabitants, and they were every day driven nearer the Irish Sea.' This driving of the Ancient Britons out of England into Wales lasted some century and a half, terminating with the Battle of Chester about A.D. 617. After this ignominious and depressing experience, the Welsh began to settle down, Cymru had begun, and all henceforth was plain sailing.

Here in Abergavenny, seventy years ago almost to the day,[4] a leading light from England, the historian, E. A. Freeman, was browbeating the 'Cambrian Archæological Association' with this doctrine of the Expulsion of the Welsh out of England into Wales; and the 'Cambrians' were taking it, all sitting down, meek as lambs.

---

4. *Arch. Camb.* (1876), 323—336.

And yet the truth is (as it was then), that there was no departure of the Romans and that there was no expulsion of Britons into Wales. The Romans are still here in every part of what was once Roman Britain, and the Britons are still here in Wales (as too in Cornwall) where they have always been. And as for the Battle of Chester in 617, it had no political significance whatsoever.

The 'Cambrians' indeed could have known better and ought to have known better, because four years previously the Welsh historian, Gweirydd ap Rhys, in his *Hanes y Brytaniaid a'r Cymry* had demonstrated that Wales had long been fully inhabited from pre-historic times. There would have been no room for refugees from England. On the ground of common sense alone the doctrine was incredible. And so he rightly declared it to be *camsyniad dybryd*, a flagrant error. But the learned men of Wales would not listen.[5]

In view of so much confusion what is one to do in order to arrive at the truth? First, we need to draw a sharp line between history and pre-history. The history of Wales begins in A.D.50, when as yet there was no Wales. The first recorded incident is the invasion of 'Flintshire' by the Roman general, Ostorius Scapula. Wales as yet was only the geographical area, which we now know by this name, containing several nations (or 'tribes' as they are called), the best known of which were the Ordovices in Central Wales and the Silures in the south-east. Secondly, we need to find a fresh line between Wales as a mere geographical area and Wales as a possible district under Roman rule, containing a population becoming self-conscious and distinct from their neighbours. Hereabouts, the very earliest beginnings of the Welsh as a nation would come to view. To find such a line might not be easy because nations do not grow in a day.

However, in A.D. 296 the emperor, Diocletian, divided the Roman Province of Britain into four small Britains, *viz*., Britannia Prima, Secunda, Flavia and Maxima. Giraldus Cambrensis discovered in the papal archives at Rome that of these four Britains Maxima was in the North, Flavia and Secunda were in the South East, whilst Britannia Prima was towards the West, including Wales and the West Country.[6] This discovery has been so far confirmed, that Britannia Prima contained the city and canton of Corinium Dobunorum (Cirencester) which was the seat of its civil governor. As Cirencester was the largest city except London in Roman Britain,

---
5. *Hanes*, i, 34. No mention is made in the *Journal of the Cambrian Archaeological Association* of the name or work of Gweirydd ap Rhys (1807—1889), till the belated reference in *Arch. Camb.* (1943), 236—37.
6. *De Invectionibus* (W. S. Davies, *Y Cymmrodor*, xxx, 130).

it would look as though it was the chief city in western Britain. There is ground also for believing that this western Britain was accounted an island in itself, an 'Island of Britain' in Britain, with the three adjacent islands of Man, Anglesey and Wight.[7]

In A.D. 369, Count Theodosius, after his victories over the Picts and other marauders, and after his restoration of the Roman Wall, and after his suppression of mutiny and discontent in the army of Britain, all of which (be it noted) he accomplished in conjunction with his able subordinate and kinsman, Magnus Maximus, proceeded to add a fifth Britain to the other four. This fifth Britain was named Valentia, and Giraldus found it to be situated beyond the Wall in Scotland. But many years ago Dr. Skene submitted that Valentia was Wales, a theory that has recently been revived[8]. Moreover, it is now suggested that the officer put in charge of Valentia or Wales, was none other than Magnus Maximus with his head-quarters at the fort of Segontium or Caer Saint in Arfon.

MAXIM WLETIC.

We come to what we may tentatively regard as the first great event in Welsh national history. It is agreed on all sides that with the Revolt of Magnus Maximus in 383 the disintegration of Roman Britain began. The North, the West and the South East began to fall apart, and their histories begin to take different directions.

This remarkable man, Magnus Maximus, acclaimed by friend and foe to have been worthy of the empire, had lived in Britain some twelve years, where he had so distinguished himself that he was hailed as emperor by the army. He proceeded almost at once to the continent, followed by the military strength of Britain. In doing this he effected two notable changes: first, he withdrew the garrison from the Roman Wall, which was now finally abandoned, leaving the North (including the Lowlands) under local military leaders; and secondly, he also withdrew the regular defences of Wales and the West Country, leaving these too in charge of friendly forces. This does not mean that he abandoned the North or that he abandoned the West (that was the last wish in the world, which either the North or the West would have entertained), but that he placed them under the protection of irregular local troops except where city militias were adequate. In consequence of this new policy, both the North and the West began very naturally to take on a certain measure of autonomy. The heads of leading local families came to the front *trwy ganiatâd Rhufeinig* 'by Roman consent' as the Welsh historian, Carnhuanawc, puts it.[9]

---

7. The 'Island of Britain' in Britain (*Notes and Queries*, 1948, p.p. 35—36).
8. Skene, *Celtic Scotland*, i, 100—3.
9. *Hanes Cymru*, 147.

In brief, at this time the Roman Province of Britain fell apart into its three natural portions — the North beyond the Humber right up to the borders of the Picts; the West, from the Irish Sea to the Channel; and the South East, *i.e.*, England south of the Humber. Of these three portions the South East was all covered with Roman cities and their territories; the North and the West not wholly so.

In the Welsh tradition Maximus is remembered as Maxim Wletic—such is his style in our oldest and best Welsh pedigrees, drawn up in the court of Howel Dda.[10] In Welsh legend he is known (but less correctly) as Maxen Wledig. On the so called Pillar of Eliseg in the Vale of Llangollen, which dates from the ninth century and which was erected by one of the kings of Powys, Maximus is said to have been (through his daughter Sevira) the father-in-law of Vortigern, who was the forbear of the kings of Powys.[11] In the Harleian Pedigrees the kings of Dyfed and of the Isle of Man trace their descent from Maximus.[12] In the earliest known draft of the Cantreds and Commotes of Wales[13] Maximus is the father of Owain king of Buallt, from whose loins (according to the Life of St. Cadog), sprang the kings of Glywysing, that extensive kingdom in the South, which once stretched westwards from the River Usk to the River Tywi and beyond.[14] In the Jesus College pedigrees[15] (our second oldest and best) one of the sons of Maximus was Constantine, who (in spite of early confusions) was long remembered to have lived in Caernarvon.[16] In these same pedigrees the kings of Cornwall trace their descent from Eudaf, the father of Elen, wife of Maximus.[17] Even in the North there survives a pedigree, which makes Octa, who afterwards, was the forbear of the kings of Kent, to have descended from Leo son of Maximus.[18] One can hardly mistake the significance of these particulars. It would appear that princes, ranging from the Lowlands of Scotland down through the Isle of Man, and through the principal divisions of Wales—west of the territoria of Deva (*Chester*),[19] Viroconium Cornoviorum (*Wroxeter*) and Venta Silurum (*Caerwent*)—and as far as Cornwall, deduced

---

10. *Nennius*, pp. 103—4.
11. *ibid.*, pp. 32—34.
12. Ped. ii., iv.
13. Hall, *Red Book of the Exchequer*, ii, 760—2; *Reports on MSS. in the Welsh Language*, ii, 939—40.
14. *Vitae Sanctorum Brittaniae*, 118; Phillimore (Owen's *Pembrokeshire*, i, 208).
15. *Y Cymmrodor*, viii, 84, ' Custenin m. Maxen.'
16. Peniarth MS. 182, *c.* 1504 (Reports on MSS. in the Welsh Language, I, iii, 1007.)
17. Jesus College Pedigrees (*Y Cymmrodor*, viii, 86).
18. Anscombe, *Eriu*, vi, 117—120.
19. The territory round Deva (Chester), later known as Westerne, and included in the kingdom of Mercia. There is no evidence that it was ever a principality of Britons as commonly assumed of this district.

their origin from Maximus through alleged sons of his, through his daughter Sevira, and through his wife's family. It would appear even as though already Wales, west of the R. Clwyd and of the R. Usk, all of it cityless, was treated as a distinct entity under the care of leaders, affiliated to Maximus.[20]

In the Welsh medieval story *Breuddwyd Maxen Wledig*, Maximus is explicitly associated with Caer Aber Saint in Arfon, which points to the Roman Fort of Segontium or Caer Saint, situated in what became later the parish of Llanbeblig. In the precious medieval tract, *Bonedd y Saint*, Peblig, the patron saint of Llanbeblig, is stationed at Caernarvon, son of Maxen Wledig, emperor of Rome, with Elen daughter of Eudaf as his mother.[21] According to Nennius a Roman Emperor of the name of Constantine lies buried at Segontium with an inscription on his tomb to the effect that he was the son of what appears to have been Magnus Maximus, only that it was read as signifying the son of one 'great, very great' and identified out of all reason with Constantine the Great. It was evidently the tomb of Constantine, son of Maximus, regarded in Arfon as having succeeded his father as 'emperor'.[22] In another Harleian pedigree there is a line of Welsh princes running back through a long list of Roman emperors to Augustus Cæsar. It could be shown that this pedigree is that of princes of Arfon, in which once again Constantine the Great has been erroneously substituted for Constantine, son of Maximus.[23]

More has come to light recently which serves to confirm and clinch the conclusion to which all this Welsh tradition points. In the document known as *Notitia Dignitatum*, compiled in its present form about A.D. 425, when Aëtius was becoming the chief power in Gaul and the West, there is found among the Palatine troops, the highest-ranked of the imperial household, a body of men called the Seguntienses. They are stationed in far-off Illyricum, but their name clearly derives from the Welsh fort of Segontium in Arfon. These (it is maintained) must have been originally the body-guard of Maxim Wletic, his household troops, the men who constituted the nucleus of that vast army, which he led out of Britain in his Gallic and Italian campaigns. They must also have been the men, who surrounded his person, when he entered Rome in the autumn of 387. Forty years later they are in Illyricum, posted among 'the Palatine auxiliaries'.[24]

---

20. 'The Origin of Cornwall' (*Notes and Queries*, 1948, pp. 289—292).
21. *Vitae Sanctorum Britanniae*..., 320—3.
22. *Nennius*, 25.
23. Ped. xvi. Lou hen map Guidgen. *cf.* Lleu and Gwydyon in the Mabinogi of Math (Ellis-Lloyd, i, 100—132).
24. C. E. Stevens (*Arch. Journal*, 1940, p. 134).

Here we find an intelligible explanation of how the Red Dragon became the symbol of Wales. Ammianus Marcellinus,[25] the last Roman historian, describes in one place how the Cæsar was recognised in battle by the purple standard of the dragon, being the Roman imperial standard. As the one and only Roman emperor, who marched out of Wales, was Maxim Wletic, the origin of the Welsh Dragon cannot but be ascribed to this event. It is a sign (if not a proof) that the inauguration of Welsh national history towards the end of the fourth century, was attended by an ebullition of Roman feeling, which persisted among the Britons of Wales for centuries. In short, it was the Red Dragon of Maxim Wletic which led the way. *Y Ddraig Goch a ddyry cychwyn.*

Maxim Wletic fell on July 28, 388. It is a day to be marked in the Welsh Kalendar. When the news reached our shores, there is evidence that the old enemies of Roman Britain, Picts, Scots, and Saxons, renewed their marauding activities.[26] It may be that the defences of Wales especially in Gwynedd and Dyfed, in which considerable bodies of Irish had settled, broke down. Among the princes affiliated to Maxim, who held ground, there is one in particular who later achieved fame and notoriety, *viz.*, Vortigern in Powys.

CUNEDDA WLEDIG.

SEVEN years after the death of Maximus, Honorius became emperor at Rome, and Stilicho his minister took in hand the pacification of Britain. It was at this juncture[27] (as is now plausibly maintained) that Cunedda Wledig with his eight sons came down from the North, from a little district on the Firth of Forth called Manaw of the Gododdin. This occurred about the turn of the century, A.D. 400. Whether they were directed to come by Stilicho or whether they came of their own accord, or both, I have for some time suggested that Cunedda assembled forces of divers elements, mostly British-speaking, who under the name of Cymry 'compatriots' assembled around Luguvallium (*Carlisle*) where they have left their name in Cumberland, if indeed they were the Cymry. From there they crossed the Irish Sea for the North Welsh coast, rounded the promontory of Lleyn for the shores of Cardigan Bay, and also doubled St. David's Head to sail up the Severn Sea, where they effected settlements in Cydweli and Gower[28]. Their object in coming was to expel the recent intruders from Ireland, which they seem to have accomplished with great effect. It may be (as I have suggested) that these were the first Cymry in Wales, the name having possibly originated thus in the North, although (as

---
25. xvi, 12,39.
26. Claudian (Monumenta Historica Britannica, ed. H. Petrie and J. Sharpe, 1848, xcvii—viii).
27. Nennius, 62, '146 years before Maelgwn reigned.'
28. *ibid*, 14.

Gweirydd ap Rhys demonstrated) it was not till much later that the Welsh in general adopted the name of Cymry as a national appellation[29]. But be this as it may, the map of Wales underwent considerable alteration as a result of Cunedda's arrival. Nine fresh principalities were established, roughly between the Dee and the Teify. These were Meirionnydd, Ceredigion, Dunoding and Afloegion in Cardigan Bay; Ysfeilion in north east Anglesey; Rhos, Rhufoniog, Dogfeiling, and Edeirnion, east of the R. Conwy. As these nine principalities lie between the far more extensive portions of Wales ruled by the descendants of Maxim Wletic, one must guard against magnifying Cunedda (as the manner is) at the expense and even to the exclusion of Maxim. Both the North and the West owed their initial autonomy to Maxim. We may, therefore, fairly regard the arrival of Cunedda as martial aid provided by the men of the North for the benefit of the men of the West. And this we may treat as the second great event in Welsh national history.[30]

At this point we need to review what was happening in England, south of the Humber, where most of the Roman cities lay. It was still being occupied by the Roman garrison. In 402 Stilicho was compelled to withdraw troops, thus weakening the Roman defence more than ever, which now fell back to cover London and the forts of the Saxon shore from the Wash to the Solent. In 406 the enfeebled garrison rebelled, and set up three usurpers in rapid succession. The last of these, known as Constantine III, proceeded to the continent (in imitation of Maximus), taking with him almost all that was left of the British army. Doubtless he believed that if Maximus could afford to leave the North and the West to fend for themselves, he likewise could venture to leave the South East. This proved disastrous. The South East was immediately infested by the continental sea-rovers, whom the Romans always grouped together under the name of *Saxones*. The cities rose in self-defence and succeeded in beating off the marauders. Then, rising in revolt against Constantine III, whom the garrison had set up, the citizens drove out all his officials, from which time such officials ceased to exist, and renewed their allegiance to Honorius, despatching letters of apology to him. He in reply forgave them for taking up arms, and urged them to proceed with their own defence, till further provision could be made. Thus in 410 by virtue of this famous Rescript of the Emperor, the South East, *i.e.*, England south of the Humber, drifted into autonomy under the rule of the cities—such autonomy as the North and West had already enjoyed for some quarter of a century.

We here arrive at a crucial period of Anglo-Welsh history, where so far our English masters have had all the say, with no sort of adequate reply from the Welsh side, nay, with no reply at all.

---

29. *Hanes*, i, 19.
30. *Nennius*, pp. 113—4.

Note then that in 410 all Roman Britain (including the Lowlands of Scotland, which were evidently within the Roman orbit) was now autonomous in its three main parts, namely, the North beyond the Humber; the West from the Irish Sea to the Channel; and the South East, which now (after the imperial rescript) comprised all the Roman cities as far as Isurium Brigantium (*Aldborough*) in Yorkshire, and as far west as Wroxeter, Caerwent, and Exeter. The lines of division between these three parts are uncertain, but it may be said in a general way that the North and the West would now mean the cityless districts. There was no breaking away from the empire on the part of any of them. They all looked to the empire as the seat of power, which was soon to be represented for them by Aëtius, the Roman minister and general in Gaul.

Note also that all the inhabitants were known in Latin and to the Romans as *Britanni*, which is commonly but misleadingly translated Britons. By the *Britanni* of Roman Britain were meant the Roman provincials, the citizens, of whatever origin.

Note this further, that the Roman cities were in a state of decay, but such as they were they adhered still to the Roman way of life. They stood for Romanitas, 'Romanity', which was the 'conservatism' of the time. But they were set in the midst of a barbarized *Britanni*, who (now that they were free) were beginning to assert themselves, slackening in what attachment they felt towards Roman traditions, including Christianity, the official religion of the empire. In other words, Barbaria was gathering strength throughout the area governed by the Roman cities, and a prolonged tension set in between it and Romanitas. This tension extended through the whole of 'England' where the cities stood, and lasted thirty three years, coming to a head in A.D. 443.

During these thirty-three years (410—443) the growing tension between Romanitas and Barbaria in England found repercussion in Wales. And here we come to the third great event in Welsh national history.

The repercussion took the form of a short but sharp struggle between two leaders, both of them nobles, Vortigern and Ambrosius. Vortigern, as we have seen, was the son-in-law of Maxim Wletic[31]. He had survived what calamities befell Wales on the death of Maximus, and was now chief ruler in Powys, his homeland being Gwrtheyrnion (in modern Radnorshire) towards the southern extremity of ancient Powys.[32] But he would seem to have got possession of the fort of Dinas Emrys in Arfon[33], which Maxim had given to Elen, Vortigern's mother-in-law. He seems also to have had a foothold in Dyfed

31. *Nennius*, pp. 32—34.
32. *ibid.*, p. 58.
33. *ibid.*, p. 65.

at Craig Gwrtheyrn on the south bank of the Teify[34]. Even in the Romano-British canton of Venta Belgarum (Winchester) a fortress bearing his name at or near Bradford-on-Avon seems to point to his presence in that quarter, where the ' Belgæ ' were re-appearing as the Gewisse[35]. In the Romano-British canton of Venta Silurum (Caerwent), his son Gwrthefyr or Vortimer held an estate at Gwrthefyriwg, now corrupted into Worthybrook, in Wonastow, Monmouthshire[36]. Briton though he was, of high Latin lineage, he favoured Barbaria (like many another noble throughout the empire at that time), as against Romanitas, with the result that he was execrated by his fellow-Britons, who, as we have seen, were pro-Roman. All the men of his nation (we are told) rose against him, for in 425 he had attained power in the West[37]. Nevertheless in 428 he allied himself with the supporters of Barbaria in the South East. His position became perilous to a degree, for he lived in constant fear not only of Picts and Scots, but (as we are told) ' of Ambrosius and a Roman attack '.

ST. GERMANUS OF AUXERRE.

The Roman attack came at once, direct from Gaul, where Aëtius was now in full power, for the very next year, 429, St. Germanus of Auxerre, great Roman ecclesiastic and famous Roman aristocrat, landed in Britain. This was his first visit. Ostensibly he came to combat the Pelagian heresy. But it is evident from the earliest traditions[38] of Wales (and Cornwall) as well as from what else we know of the career of this august personage, that his mission was also (if not mainly) political. In fact, his mission in the West was plainly to dislodge Vortigern. We find him in northern Powys, where he succeeds in raising Cadell Ddyrnllug to the Powysian throne, who is no other than Cateŷrn, the son of Vortigern, who evidently opposed his father and favoured Romanitas. He next accosts Vortigern, face to face, apparently in Arfon, the saint being accompanied by all the clergy of the Britons. Vortigern flies before him to his homeland of Gwrtheyrnion. St. Germanus pursues him; and again Vortigern flies, this time to his citadel in Dyfed, where he perishes on the banks of the Teify, A.D.430.

With the death of Vortigern the cause of Barbaria and paganism ended among the Britons, whilst Romanitas with Christianity prevailed under the leadership of Ambrosius Aurelianus, *i.e.*, Emrys Wledig, who (as we are told), born in the purple, was ' king

34. *ibid.*, p. 69.
35. Wirtgernesburg (William of Malmesbury, i.2.).
36. *Book of Llan Dâv*, 201. ' Gwrthebiriuc.'
37. *Nennius*, 48 and 31.
38. These taken from a lost Book of St. Germanus by Rhun son of Urien, who flourished c.626, and inserted by Nennius in his History, 32—35, 39, 47. *Arch. Camb.* (1937), pp. 64—85.

among all the kings of the British nation'[39]. In other words, Romanitas triumphed in Wales and Cornwall as against Barbaria, whereas (as we shall see) the opposite occurred in England. The mind of Roman Britain diverged thus early in the fifth century to become a Roman and Christian mind in the West, and a non-Roman and non-Christian mind in the East. This explains in large measure how it was that the *Britanni* of the East came to apply the name 'Welsh' to the *Britanni* of the West, the word 'Welsh' being the common Teutonic name, found all over Europe for 'Romans'.

The *tranquillitas* effected by St. Germanus was accompanied by a general settlement of the country under the rule of Emrys Wledig. This appears from the fact that (as we are told) he placed Pasgen, son of Vortigern, in charge of Gwrtheyrnion and Buallt[40]. It seems clear that at this time the little principalities of Wales, with the names of which we are so familiar, were finally fixed, and the rule of leading families confirmed, especially those of Maxim Wletic and Cunedda Wledig. In addition to the principalities I have already enumerated, I may now mention Brycheiniog[41], the portion assigned to the half-Irish Brychan; also the two, which are called after Roman towns, namely, Erging or Archenfield in Herefordshire, west of the Wye, so named after the Roman town of Ariconium (*Weston under Penyard*); and Gwent, so named after the city of Venta Silurum or Caerwent. These two are the only ones in Wales named after Roman towns. Neither of them came under the rule of the stocks of Maxim or Cunedda.

I would here draw attention to this salient fact, that not a single principality of Britons, such as I have enumerated, can be proved to have existed at any time or in any shape eastwards beyond the territorium of Deva (*Chester*) or the canton of Viroconium Cornoviorum (*Wroxeter*) or east of the R. Wye. Within half a century from the Revolt of Maximus in 383, we find the Wales we know to-day already fashioned, distinct from the North and distinct from the South East. The limits provided by Offa of Mercia four centuries later were clearly the traditional eastern boundaries of the Britons, to whose protection Maximus committed the care of 'Wales'. The *Britanni*, who occupied it, of whatever origin, appeared under this one common name of Britons or Brythoniaid.

The tension in England south of the Humber between Romanitas and Barbaria increased with calamities of various kinds. It became necessary for St. Germanus to pay a second visit to the island, which occurred, as recently shewn, not later than 444[42]. Ostensibly again he came to combat a revival of the Pelagian heresy, but once

---

39. *Nennius*, 48.
40. *ibid.*
41. *Vitae Sanctorum Britanniae.* . . . p. 313.
42. *English Historical Review*, July 1941, p. 365 ('Gildas Sapiens' by C. E. Stevens).

more it is evident that he was commissioned to effect a tranquillity in the South East, such as he had successfully achieved some twelve years before in the West (and indeed in the North). It was in every respect in accordance with the well known policy of Aëtius to preserve Roman honour by appeasement. We possess strictly contemporary evidence that by 443 Britains, which up to this time had been torn by various calamities, were now reduced under the jurisdiction of the English. The words are these, taken from the ' Gallic Chronicle of 452', and quoted by Gweirydd ap Rhys[43] who claims to have been the first to place them before Welsh readers—

[A.D.442-3] Brittaniæ usque ad hoc tempus variis cladibus eventibusque la[cera]tæ in dicionem Saxonum rediguntur.

(Britains up to this time torn by various disasters and other occurrences are reduced under the jurisdiction of Saxons.)

This statement needs careful handling, but its meaning is clear. It signifies that the area, which contained the Roman cities, having become autonomous, had undergone the throes of internal changes, wherein the chief constituents of its population, to wit, those described by the Romans as ' Saxons ' with their supporters and sympathizers, had come to the forefront. The *Britanni* in this area were already barbarized or as the Romans might say ' Saxonized', which *fait accompli* was recognised by Aëtius and doubtless confirmed by him in accordance with his usual well known general policy of appeasement. As Roman Britain had never broken with the empire, and as tranquillity had already been established in the West and in the North, this great event in 443 can only refer to the South East, and must have been due to a diplomatic arrangement under Aëtius through the instrumentality of St. Germanus. Henceforth the *Britanni* of the South East re-appear as ' Saxons', just as those of the West re-appear as Britons, and those of the North as Nordi and Gwŷr y Gogledd, ' Men of the North'.

GEMITUS BRITANNORUM.

Three years after this settlement in the South East, a famous Letter was sent out of Britain, in which the whole province joined. It was addressed to Aëtius, the great Roman minister in Gaul, and was an appeal for martial assistance against the Picts and Scots, who were bent on an invasion of the land on a grand scale. Two bits of the Letter survive, and are as follows[44]:—

(a) To Agitius, thrice consul, the groans of the *Britanni*.
(b) The Barbarians drive us back to the Sea, the Sea drives us back to the Barbarians, Between these two modes of death we are either killed or drowned.

---

43. *Hanes*, i., 170.
44. *de excidio*, 20.

The Letter was sent in A.D. 446 and is generally known as *gemitus Britannorum*. Up till 1943 it was understood by everybody (including myself) as signifying ' the groans of the Britons'. Understood as such it was a baffling document, and the attempts to explain it were multifarious. Many would try to explain it away. In 1943[45]. the truth came to light. It was not the groans of the Britons (nor could it have been), but the groans of the Britannians, *i.e.*, all the provincials of Roman Britain of whatever origin, ' Saxons ' as well as ' Britons'. The very name of Aêtius (to distinguish the initial vowels) is spelt in English fashion. This Letter in itself disposes once and for all of the story, as first told by Bede, of the Anglo-Saxon Conquest of Britain with its attendant corollary of the Expulsion of the Britons into Wales and Cornwall.

ARTHUR.

No aid was forthcoming in response to this Letter, but it is evident that the *Britanni* were encouraged to fight for themselves, which they did with great effect in a series of what were esteemed brilliant victories, whereby they not only cleared the Picts and Scots out of the Roman province, but also recovered the Lowlands of Scotland right up to the Pictish borders. These victories, to which I draw particular attention, for their significance seems to have been entirely overlooked, are recorded as follows[46] :—

"And then it was for the first time that [the citizens] began to inflict slaughters on their foes, who for many years had been plundering in the land. They trusted not in man, but in God."

There can be no manner or shadow of doubt that these victories over the Picts and Scots are those, in which Arthur, although not named, distinguished himself. This record, therefore, disposes of the subsequent belief (as found in Nennius[47]) that Arthur's enemies were the Saxons and that he was the chief protagonist at ' Badon Hill'. Here in fact we find the historic Arthur in his true setting, who is seen to be a Roman provincial, in the Roman service, commissioned to direct Britannic forces, not against invading Saxons (there were none), but against plundering Picts and Scots. And with Arthur, engaged in the same task, we shall find Octa and Ebissa[48], Frisian or Jutish leaders, also in the Roman service.

As the name ' Arthur ' is the rule-right equivalent in Welsh of the Latin *Artorius*, it cannot be doubted that he belonged to the Britons and that his charge was westwards rather than towards the east. This is confirmed by the statement that he fought ' along

---

45. *Arch. Camb.* (1944), pp. 119—20.
46. *de excidio*, 20; N. & .Q (1948),508.
47. *Nennius*, 56.
48. *ibid.*, 38, 56, 58.

with the kings of the Britons'. Not a king himself nor is he ever styled *gwledig*, i.e., ruler in a Roman sense, his office must have been of an exceptional character. As his *floruit* synchronizes with the 'transit' of Octa into Kent, their commissions were doubtless from the same source (ultimately of course Aëtius), that as Octa was finally posted in Kent in some exceptional capacity, so Arthur's activities in some corresponding capacity were to the west and north. Many years ago Professor John Rhys proffered the illuminating suggestion[49], couched in carefully worded terms, that Arthur 'falls readily into the place and position of a successor of the Count of Britain', to which I now venture to add that Octa likewise 'falls readily into the place and position of a successor' of the Count of the Saxon shore.

In consequence of these victories Roman Britain grew prosperous, even wealthy, as never before. The inhabitants, now appeased and flushed with their triumphs, increased steadily in number, both 'Saxons' and 'Britons' within their respective bounds, until the land was unable to contain them (not however without occasional raids of Picts and Scots), the 'Britons' to the west in Wales and 'Cornwall', and the 'Saxons'[50] to the east in the area of the cities, whilst beyond the Humber right up to the border of the Picts were 'Britons' and 'Saxons' grouped together as Nordi, Gwŷr y Gogledd, 'Men of the North'.

And now (so we are told) it was that 'kings were being anointed',[51] a statement specially applicable to the area of the cities, which were falling into decay. Of the pedigrees of these kings, running back into Roman times, we have ample evidence in all parts.

Moreover, with the triumph of Barbaria, the nomenclature of Britain throughout the territoria of the various cities underwent an extensive change, preserving traditional boundaries, however, in remarkably recognizable fashion (which tells its own story) even to this day under new appellations.

I subjoin the following scheme, based on the findings of Giraldus Cambrensis, to illustrate this.

---

49. *Celtic Britain*, 239.
50. *de excidio*, 21.
51. *ibid*. The anointing of Kings at their coronation after the end of the Western Empire must have been introduced into Britain at about the same time as it was into Spain, *i.e.* in the 7th century (C. Delisle Burns, *The First Europe*, 291), so that the author of the *de excidio* transferred into the 5th century a custom which had only recently been started in Europe when he was writing in 708.

BRITANNIA PRIMA.

DUMNONII : = 'Devon.'
  Isca Dumnoniorum (*Exeter*)

DUROTRIGES : = 'Dorset.'
  Durnovaria Durotrigum (*Dorchester*)

BELGÆ : = Gewisse.
  Venta Belgarum (*Winchester*)

DOBUNI : = Hwicce.
  Corinium Dobunorum (*Cirencester*)
  Glevum (*Gloucester*), colonia.

SILURES : = Gwent.
  Venta Silurum (*Caerwent*)

CORNOVII :
  Viroconium Cornoviorum (*Wroxeter*)

[(a) To the above add all the rest of Wales, the land of the Britons.
  (b) From the canton of the Dumnonii were detached, possibly during the first visit of St. Germanus, both Cornwall and portions of north Devon and Somerset, also occupied by Britons. N & Q (1948), 289—292.
  (c) The Cornovii round Wroxeter did not re-appear under a single name; they split into a number of small units. But Deva (Chester) retained its territorium.
  (d) For evidence that Britannia Prima was known as an 'Island of Britain' with the three adjacent islands of Man, Anglesey, and Wight, see *Notes & Queries.*, Vol., 193, No. 2, pp. 35-6.]

BRITANNIA SECUNDA.

TRINOBANTES : = East Saxons.
  Camulodunum (Colchester), colonia.

CATUVELLAUNI : = Middle Saxons
  Verulamium (St. Albans), municipium.
  Augusta, alias Londinium (London)

ATREBATES : = West Saxons.
  Calleva Atrebatum (Silchester)

REGNENSES : = South Saxons.
  Noviomagus Regnensium (Chichester)

CANTIACI : = Cantware.
  Durovernum Cantiacorum (Canterbury)

[The Angles of Britannia Secunda assumed the Roman appellation of Saxons to distinguish themselves from their fellow-Angles, thus preserving the memory of the old Roman division.

The advent of Octa in Kent from the Lowlands made that canton Frisian or Jutish. See N. & Q., Vol., 193, No. 25, pp. 542-4.]

BRITANNIA FLAVIA.

Iceni = East Angles.
Venta Icenorum (Caistor by Norwich).

Coritani : = Middle Ages.
Ratae Coritanorum (Leicester)   with the Lindisse
Lindum (Lincoln), Colonia.

BRITANNIA MAXIMA.

Brigantes : = Nordanhymbri
Isurium Brigantium (Aldborough).

VALENTIA.

Dumnonii :
Ystrad Clud (Clydesdale).

Novantae :
Aeron (Ayr), Rheged.

Selgovae :
Goddau (Forest).

Votadini :
Manaw, Eiddyn, Bernicia.

The increasing prosperity of what was once Roman Britain is confirmed by Procopius of Cæsarea[52] shortly after A.D.550. He provides a confused account of two islands, viz., Brittia over against Gaul and Britannia to the west over against Spain. The last is evidently Britannia Prima regarded as an "Island of Britain" in Britain. But it is equally evident that in the following quotation he is referring to Roman Britain as a whole:

> The island of Britain contains three very populous nations, each of which has a king over it. The names borne by these nations are Angles, Frisians, and Britons, the last having the same name as the island. So numerous are these

---

52. *de bello Gothico*, iv, 20.

nations that every year great numbers with their wives and children migrate to the Franks, and the Franks give them dwellings in that part of their Island which seems most bare of men. From which fact they say that they make a claim to this island. So that indeed not long since the king of the Franks [*i.e.*, Theudebert, 534—548], when he despatched some of his own people on an embassy to the emperor Justinian [527—565] at Byzantium, sent with them some men of the Angles, making a display, as if the island also, was ruled by him.

Procopius clearly obtained this information direct from the very Angles, who visited the court of Justinian. It is therefore all the more significant. It contains the first-known mention of the Angles in Britain, who gave their name to 'England', a sure indication that Angles was the native name. In fact, Angles and Saxons were convertible terms, the former insular and native, the latter Roman and literary. Procopius evidently heard the native name only. The Frisians must have been those whom Bede over a century and a half later called Jutes. It is to be noted too that the above quotation contains the first-known mention of the *Britanni* of the west as 'Britons'. It may be said at once in anticipation that it is impossible to square Bede's speculation as to the origins of the English with this earlier and less sophisticated evidence of Procopius.

EPISTOLA GILDÆ.

Some ten years prior to Procopius's testimony, St. Gildas[53] wrote an open letter of rebuke to the secular and ecclesiastical rulers of " Britannia " which he names six times (even speaks of it as ' the whole island ')[54] and describes as *patria* ' fatherland ' and its inhabitants as *cives*, citizens. But he does not once name the *Britanni* nor does he make any reference to Picts, Scots, or Saxons, or to any heathenism in the land, only to its wickedness, which is his sole theme. By Britannia he means not the whole British isle (nor could he have meant it), but only a portion, inclusive of Wales and the West Country, for the land is clearly Christian, and he addresses by name five kings, all of whom can be identified and located. They are Constantine of Damnonia ' Devon '; Aurelius Caninus [of Cornwall]; Vortiporius of Dyfed; Cuneglas of Dineirth near Llandudno in Rhos; and Maglocunus of Anglesey ' the island dragon'. In brief, by Britannia he means that ' Island of Britain ' in Britain, to which Procopius in his confused way refers.

---

53. *Chronica Minora*, iii, 25—85; Gildas (Cymmrodorion Record Series, No. 3, 1899) by Hugh Williams, with translations, &c.
54. *Epistola Gildae*, 93.

St. Gildas was a cleric, apparently a monk, who at the time of writing, dissatisfied with the world around him, including the monastic world, to which he himself belonged, was anxious to become an anchorite[55]. He is made in an early Breton document[56] to have been a disciple of St. Illtud at Llantwit Major. But this is not so. Gildas from the first was a disciple of St. Cadog, in whose great monastery at Llancarfan he is later heard of as Cadog's confessor. Among the treasures at Llancarfan were Gildas's miraculous Bell, also his 'Missal book' known as *Evangelium Gildæ*, written by him on the island of Flatholm in the Bristol Channel, on which island too it could be shewn that he wrote his *Epistola*.

And here I would draw attention to what is either unknown or completely ignored, that St. Gildas was not a Briton, but a Pict. Nor was he a man of high rank, his father being the leader of a troop or horde of Pictish raiders, kilted barbarians, of whom the author of the *de excidio* states that they preferred to cover their villainous faces with hair rather than the less decent parts of their bodies with clothing. Such was Gildas's father, *Caw Prydyn*, Caw of Pictland, who made a descent on Arglud or Clydeside, where he fell under the influence of St. Cadog, who was digging the foundations of a new monastery, probably at Cambuslang in Lanarkshire, of which church St. Cadog is still patron. Here in Arglud St. Gildas was born[57].

THE MEN OF THE NORTH.

Having now reached the mid-sixth century, it will be necessary at this point to leave Wales for the moment and to treat briefly on the affairs of the North; *i.e.* the country beyond the territorium of Deva (*Chester*) and the Humber, including the Lowlands of Scotland between the Roman Walls.

When Cunedda Wledig and his sons left Manaw of the Gododdin, the protection of that side of the Lowlands was left to the people who held the fortress of Inchkeith, an island in the Firth of Forth[58]. These were the Frisians or Jutes, who later held many districts from the 'Frisian Shore' on the Firth of Forth across the Lowlands down to Dumfries 'the Fort of the Frisians'. Maximus would seem to have left these in the charge of a general, named Leo, affiliated to him in a pedigree which has fortunately survived. Leo's grandson was Octa, the contemporary of Arthur. To the

---

55. Williams, *op.cit*, 161—2.
56. Wrmonoc's Life of St. Paul Aurelian (A.D. 884).
57. *Vitae Sanctorum Britanniae*.... 84, 94, 96.
58. Inchkeith was the fortress in the Forth to the east corresponding to Dumbarton to the west.

south and east of these Frisians (if indeed they themselves were not of the Frisians) were the Bernicians, ruled by princes who continued for some time to acknowledge allegiance to the descendants of Octa in Kent; and still further south were the Deirans (who also themselves, may have been of the Frisians), one of whose princes, Soemil[59] by name, had in the early fifth century (about the time of St. Germanus's first visit to Britain) detached Deira from Bernicia. I know of no Britons in the north of England at this time unless it be around Carlisle, where I have submitted there may have been Cymry. Britons however, were strong in the Western Lowlands, under the rule of two leading families, that of Coel Odebog of Aeron ' Ayr ' (including Kyle in modern Ayrshire) and that of Ceredig Wledig of Alclud or Dumbarton in Strathclyde, ' the fort of the Britons'. Along the north of Solway Firth in Galloway was Rheged with its fortress at Dun Ragit in Wigtonshire; to the north-east of Rheged was Goddau, the great wood still known in part as Forest; and beyond that the small district of Manaw of the Gododdin (*i.e.*, of the ancient nation or ' tribe ' known as the Votadini) with another small district called Eiddyn to the east of it including Carriden and Edinburgh. To the north of Rheged was Aeron ' Ayr ', and beyond that Ystrad Clud or Strathclyde with its strong fortress at Dumbarton, where on the Clyde the Britons stood on the defence against the Picts as the Frisians stood at Inchkeith on the Forth.

William of Malmesbury[60] has preserved a tradition, which could hardly have been invented, that Northumbrian princes acknowledged the overlordship of the kings of Kent, who were descended from Octa. And this continued till 547, when Ida, a prince of the Bernicians, cast off Kentish supremacy, making Bamborough his chief fortress. This revolt of Ida caused repercussion throughout the North. The country between the Tweed and the Forth including Manaw and Eiddyn, combined under an unidentified prince described as half-pagan, namely, Lleuddin Luyddog[61], ' of the hosts ' who left his name in Lleuddinion or Lothian. Aelle, king of Deira, doubtless took precautions. The Britons attacked Ida under a leader, otherwise unknown, Eudeyrn,[62] doubtless of the stock of Coel Odebog. No particulars are given, but Ida died in 559 and Bernicia fell straightway under the rule of Aelle of Deira.

After some years the Britons renewed their attacks against the sons of Ida. They marched under four kings, Urien Rheged, Gwallog, and Morgan, all of the stock of Coel, and Rhydderch of Strathclyde[63].

---

59. *Nennius*, 81. Samlesbury, south of the river Ribble in Lancashire may take its name from Soemil.
60. *De gestis regum*, i. 3.
61. Lleuddin of the Hosts, the *Leudonus* of the old fragmentary Life of Kentigern. (*Arch. Camb.* 1930, p. 323).
62. *Nennius*, 62 Outigern, *i.e.* Eudeyrn for 'Dutigern'.
63. *Nennius*, 63.

These led their men in forays right across the Lowlands, and also made great expeditions into North England. Urien Rheged is said to have been for a time ' ruler of Catraeth ' (supposed to be Catterick) and Gwallog would seem to have penetrated still further south and to have formed the small principality of Elmet near Leeds, for doubtless the Ceredig[64], whom Edwin afterwards expelled from that district, was his son. But there is no evidence that these British raiders from the Lowlands ever formed a terrene connection with the Britons of Wales.

It was at this time that there was a notable outburst of patriotic poetry among the Britons of the North, among their poets being Taliesin and Aneirin, some of whose works have survived[65]. The former sang to and of Urien Rheged and his son Owain and other princes, including (it would appear) Rhun son of Maelgwn Gwynedd; the latter wrote *Y Gododdin*, a more fanciful work, though one need not question the raid to Catraeth, of which it treats. Morover, well-known British saints hail from that quarter at this time, such as Kentigern of Glasgow and Beuno of Clynnog in Arfon, both grandsons of Lleuddin of Lothian. Traditions of the North are known to have been preserved in the communities of Beuno in Gwynedd[66]. One may also mention Rhun, son of Urien, a priest, who is said to have baptized Edwin of Northumbria[67], and who is reported to have been a collector of historical memoranda[68].

Ethelfrith, grandson of Ida, is extolled by Bede[69] as the foremost harasser of the Britons, who conquered more territories from them than any other, driving them out and supplanting them. But Bede, who was given to much wishful thinking does not specify the conquered districts, which certainly did not include Elmet, lying on (if not within) his borders. Ethelfrith, indeed, won a notable victory over Aidan, king of the Scots, in 603, which Aidan was no friend of the Britons and was remembered by them as Aeddan Fradog[70] ' the treacherous '. He also won the Battle of Chester in 617 (to which our historians attach such significance), when Selyf of Powys and Cadwal of Rhos fell with many hundreds of monks from Bangor Iscoed, but otherwise its results were naught, for he perished shortly after in the battle by the R. Idle.

Edwin, his successor, was another great raider, who invaded Man and Anglesey. He was opposed by Cadwallon of Gwynedd and Penda of Mercia, and fell in the Battle of Hatfield, A.D. 632. After

---

64. *Nennius*, p. 81, n 6.
65. *Nennius*, 62.
66. *Ancient Laws of Wales*, i. 106.
67. *Nennius*, 63.
68. *Arch. Camb.*, 1937, pp. 64—85.
69. *Historia ecclesiastica gentis Anglorum*, i, 34.
70. *Vitae Sanctorum Britanniae* . . . 315.

Cadwallon's death in the following year, Oswald, son of Ethelfrith, succeeded to the throne of the Northumbrians, with whose death in 642 Oswy his brother became king in Bernicia. With Oswy, we close this brief account of affairs in the North, because it would appear that he entered on all the possessions of Urien Rheged in virtue of his marriage with Rhiainfellt, great-granddaughter of Urien[71], and that these possessions possibly included the fortress of Inchkeith in the Firth of Forth, to which on one occasion he retired as his last stronghold before Penda's attack[72].

THE CONFLICT WITH CANTERBURY.

In the meantime Pope Gregory the Great had sent a band of monks under Augustine to convert the English. The missionaries landed in Kent in A.D. 597 and within a few weeks, Ethelbert, king of the Kentish folk, was baptized. That same year Augustine was consecrated ' Archbishop of the English[73] '.

The following year Augustine wrote to the Pope to inquire how he was to deal with the bishops whom he found in Britain, and Gregory replied that he committed them to Augustine's care. This however applied only to Augustine personally, not to his successors. This point would seem to have been kept in the background. It was not intended by the Pope that the Church throughout the whole of Britain should be subject to Canterbury, but only to Augustine as long as he lived[74].

St. Augustine met in conference the bishops and doctors of the Britons, apparently at Cricklade on the borders of the Gewisse. He told them of certain matters, wherein the Britons were not at one with the rest of the Church. They did not keep Easter at the proper time, and there were other things. A long disputation followed. The Britons refused to fall in, but asked for a second conference. It is evident that feelings were running high.

The second conference was at Chester. In three matters, said Augustine, I ask you to comply : (1) to keep Easter at the due time ; (2) to complete the ministry of baptism ; and (3) to join in evangelizing the English heathen. They answered that they would do none of these things, *nor would they receive him as their archbishop*[75]. This last constituted the sting of the argument. Was Canterbury to be supreme over Wales ? Augustine died in 605, and with him ended Canterbury's jurisdiction (such as it was) over the Welsh.

---

71. *Nennius*, 57.
72. *Nennius* p. 82. The parenthesis which connects *cc*. 64, 65, should close with the words Atbret Judeu.
73. Bede, *Historia ecclesiastica* . . . . .i, 23.
74. *ibid*, 27.
75. *ibid*., ii, 2.

Wales held out till 768[76] when at the persuasion of Elfoddw, 'archbishop in Gwynedd', who was able to convince the Britons from Pope Gregory's own letter, published by Bede in 731, that the archbishops of Canterbury after Augustine had no jurisdiction over them, it yielded. But the long dispute, lasting over a century and a half, created considerable bitterness, as exemplified in the writings of Aldhelm and Bede. It is questionable whether it has ever conpletely subsided or even whether it may not somehow revive.

It was and is a grievous error to suppose that the British protest against Augustine of Canterbury was aimed at the Papacy.

DE EXCIDIO BRITANNIÆ.

So far, we have seen that the course of Welsh History, as too that of Cornwall and the North, is traceable enough from the Revolt of Maximus in 383, when these parts began to drift into autonomy; and likewise, that no less traceable is the history of the rest of Roman Britain, the South East, the area containing the Roman Cities, ever since under Aëtius in 443, it came under the jurisdiction of the English. Nor would these histories have been other than traceable (indeed they would have been far more so) were it not for a cloud of obfuscation thrown upon the narrative by the publication in A.D. 708 of a little book professing to give an account of the Island of Britain ever since Maximus had left[77].

This little book, *de excidio Britanniæ* 'of the loss of Britain' is the fountain-head of the familiar story of the Anglo-Saxon Conquest of Britain together with the Expulsion of the Britons into Wales and Cornwall. Upon it, the whole story, as quoted and expanded by Bede, rests. No one ever heard of such a thing prior to the appearance of this work, and no one has ever been able to tell the tale apart from it. As this single book falls (as fall it must) every history of England ever written falls with it. And I say without any misgiving that until this book is understood for what it is, the Welsh nation will continue to be exposed as it is today, unjustly, unreasonably and without any basis whatsoever in history, to a spirit of defeatism.

Although arranged with meticulous care, the *de excidio* proves upon close examination to be a puzzling production. Its author was evidently a *Britannus*, *i.e.*, a man of Britain, a provincial, or

---

76. *Nennius*, p. 94.
77. For a fresh translation of the *de excidio*, see *Nennius's History of the Britons* (S.P.C.K., 1938) pp. 122—153. Giles's translation appears in *Six Old English Chronicles*, pp. 299—313. For a Welsh translation see *O Lygad y Ffynnon* (1899) by John Owen Jones, B.A., Bala., pp. 107—124.

(as he would term it) *civis*, a citizen. Only twice does he name the *Britanni* (the *Brittones* not at all), and then only in quotations, in one of which at least he misunderstands the term. His attitude towards them is contemptuous. *O desperabilem crudamque mentis hebitudinem !* He is hostile to the Picts and Scots, and particularly so to the *Saxones*, but curiously enough by these last he seems to be referring only to the Jutes of Hampshire and Wight, who by treacherous rebellion had filched these parts from the old Romano-British canton of Venta Belgarum (Winchester), whose inhabitants now called themselves the Gewisse.

It was his belief that the whole Island of Britain had been under Roman rule until the Revolt of Maximus. He reasoned therefore that the Picts of the Highlands must have invaded Britain from over-seas after the 'withdrawal of the Romans'. He fixed the time of their settlements in Pictland subsequent to the victories (that is, those of Arthur) which followed upon the Appeal of Aëtius in 446. This is not history, but the reasoning is intelligible.

A considerable interval elapsed, when for the first time *Saxones* were ' admitted into the island'. One is left with the impression that no Englishman had ever before set foot on British soil. Obviously, this too is not history, but its meaning and significance need to be unravelled. It would seem (if I may anticipate) that his ' Island of Britain' has here become that ' Island of Britain' in Britain, to which Procopius seems to refer and which is identifiable with the Britannia Prima of Diocletianic times, and that the admission of Jutes into this ' Island' and their subsequent rebellion and savagery he treated as a first-coming of the English into Britain at large.

The *de excidio* consists of 26 small sections, including a table of contents and a formal ending It can easily be read at a single sitting. It is found inserted into the Epistle of Gildas the Pict (*Gildas Albanius* as he is sometimes styled) ; and for this reason its authorship is commonly ascribed to him. The *de excidio*, however, betrays no affection for the Picts, and dates itself as much later than the days of Gildas Albanius. On its own shewing it was written 193 years after its first-coming of *Saxones*, which last is made to have occurred no small interval after the Letter to Aëtius in 446. For exactly 150 years the *Saxones* were in the aggressive ; then they met with a decisive check at the famous Siege of the Badonic Hill, which took place in the year of the author's birth ; and the author was 43 when he was writing. From these details, carefully provided in the book itself, its date of composition can be calculated to the very year. For fortunately the Siege of the Badonic Hill, which must on the evidence have occurred in the seventh century, is given in the Welsh *Annales*[78] as

---

78. *Nennius*, p. 91.

having been fought in A.D. 665. And so we find that by his first-coming of the *Saxones* he means the arrival of the Jutes in A.D.514[79], who were admitted into the Romano-British canton of Winchester by its ' proud tyrant ' and his councillors. This canton stretched from Portsmouth Harbour right across Hampshire, Wiltshire, and Somerset to the Bristol Channel containing the cities of Aquæ Sulis (Bath) and Ischalis by the R. Axe, in addition to Winchester, and including the Isle of Wight. [This canton, be it noted, would have been at the south east corner of that ' Island of Britain ' in Britain, mentioned above.]

The Jutes came in three ships and were later joined by a second gang in more ships. After a while these two gangs of Jutes rebelled against their ' good hosts ' and overran the canton of the Belgæ (or Gewisse as they were now called) as far as the Bristol Channel and, took permanent possession of ' Hampshire ' and the Isle of Wight. From this time the Jutes constituted one of the elements—the others were the Gewisse of ' Wiltshire ', The West Saxons of ' Berkshire ' and the Britons of ' Somerset ' —of what was to become the Kingdom of Wessex as consolidated under Ceadwalla and Ine (685—726). But they proved a very unruly element, a thorn in the side of their neighbours for exactly 150 years (514—664), when at long last they were brought into line at the Siege of the Badonic Hill. This battle, therefore, fought in 665 was no victory of ever-retreating Britons over ever-advancing Saxons, nor had it anything whatever to do with Arthur. But certainly to the author of the *de excidio* it might pass for a Britannic victory, *i.e.*, of *Britanni*, men of Britain, over a community of intractable intruders from the sea.

This arrival of Jutes in 514, joined a little later by a second batch of Jutes, is the one and only *adventus Saxonum* recorded in the *de excidio*. Its author knew of none other, from which it follows that his *Britanni*, his *cives* ' citizens', were the provincials of Roman Britain including those long ' *Saxonized* ' who in 443 had come *in dicionem Saxonum*. And so even the *de excidio* provides evidence (were more evidence required) that the story of the Anglo-Saxon conquest with the expulsion of the Britons into Wales and Cornwall is a myth.

BEDE.

The earliest-known writer to refer to the *de excidio* is Bede, who quotes passages from it in his larger chronicle in 725 and bases his account of an Anglo-Saxon conquest of Britain upon it in his *Ecclesiastical History* in 731[80].

---

79. Anglo-Saxon Chronicle [A], 514.
80. *Historia ecclesiastica.* i, 14—16, 22.   *Arch. Camb.* (1944), 115-6.

Bede, as is well known, was animated by adverse feelings, racial as well as ecclesiastical, against the Britons, which was unfortunate for so pre-eminent a historian. For Bede was the greatest historian of his age, 'the Father of English History'. He was also a great Christian. He was also a great Englishman. Believing that the *de excidio* was written by Gildas Albanius in the sixth century, not knowing, not even suspecting that its author was a contemporary of his own, he studied it with close attention, when in the last decades of his life it came his way, as his chief, if not his sole insular authority for Britannic events in the fifth century. He studied it too not without personal satisfaction. The story of the three keels kindled his imagination to launch forth into 'picturesque writing', where his patriotism and anti-British bias had full play.

Nevertheless, Bede has not escaped the censure he merits. Lappenburg[81] says that his 'glaring deficiency in historic criticism has never been duly attended to'. This is still true, and not least in his manipulation of the account of the first arrival of *Saxones* in Britain as given in the *de excidio* (the story of the two Jutish gangs)—his bold assertions, unwarranted assumptions, mis-dating of events and misleading speculations. It is amazing how Dr. Plummer[82], who in another connection says of Bede that he 'inserts as facts explanations of his own', failed to note how Bede surpassed himself in this respect in his paraphrase of these sections of the *de excidio*, which constitute the basis of English history as taught in our schools and universities. For (explain it as you will) our scholastics invariably minimize the transformation effected by Bede in the telling of this story, a story other than which he had nothing to go on.

It is Bede who says that the English first landed in Britain about 449. It is Bede, who makes Vortigern to have been King of the Britons and Ruler of southern Britain. It is Bede who states definitely that the *Saxones* came from abroad. It is Bede who says that Vortigern gave them a place wherein to settle. It is Bede who says that after landing the *Saxones* won a victory over the Picts. It is Bede who says that after this victory they sent reports of it to the continent with particulars as to 'the fertility of the island' and 'the cowardice of the Britons'. It is Bede who tells that on the reception of this news, a stronger fleet with larger numbers arrived, who also received a place to inhabit, with promise of military pay. Verily, Bede cannot be excused of the charge made against him by Lappenberg that 'for his love of the legendary' and for his 'fascinating descriptive powers', he 'may not inaptly be called the Walter Scott of the eighth century'[83].

---

81. Lappenberg, *England under the Anglo-Saxons* (Thorpe's translation), 26.
82. Plummer's *Bede*, I, xlvi.
83. Lappenberg, 148.

Moreover, at this point, Bede gives a startling turn to his story. The two Jutish gangs, who at first were ' the nation of the Angles or Saxons' now become 'of the three most powerful peoples of Germany, to wit, Saxons, Angles, Jutes', who crossed the ocean from their ancestral seats on the continent ; with Hengist and Horsa as their alleged first leaders, who landed in [Kent]; who were followed by eager swarms of their various stocks, striking terror into British hearts ; who effected a temporary alliance with the Picts, preparatory to turning against their British allies—of all which there is not a word or a hint in the authority which he follows, and he had no other.

Bede now returns to the *de excidio*, that is, to the story of the two Jutish gangs, who, having in the meantime, undergone a sea-change, have become 'three most powerful peoples of Germany to wit, Saxons, Angles, Jutes'; how they ask for more food and liquor, threatening rebellion if such were not forthcoming ; how they followed up their threats with deeds ; how they 'ravaged almost the whole surface of the perishing island from the eastern sea to the western ' ; how the Britons after having been exterminated or driven oversea or into the mountains rallied under Ambrosius Aurelianus ; how they then fought on equal terms with the invaders right up to the year of the Siege of the Badonic Hill, which (to crown the whole of this fantasy and, as Lappenberg says[84],' through one of those singular hallucinations under which he occasionally labours') he dates as having occurred ' about the 44th year after their arrival in Britain ' !

Nor is it possible to square Bede's much-advertised guesses as to the origin of the English with the plain evidence of Procopius nearly two centuries earlier. Bede in 731, working backwards from the known to the unknown—that facile but most dangerous method—makes them to have consisted of three nations, Jutes, Saxons, Angles : the Jutes in Kent, ' Hampshire' and Wight; the Saxons from Harwich to Portsmouth Harbour ; and all the rest Angles. But Procopius 554 found them to consist of two nations only, Angles and Frisians. To the Romans all of these would have been lumped together under the name *Saxones*, but among themselves the distinction was clearly between Angles and Frisians (Angles and Saxons being convertible terms for one and the same people), the Frisians being those known later to Bede as Jutes. Bede found in his day a people living in Jutland with a name very like his *Iutæ* and also a district in Jutland called *Angel* separated by an uninhabited waste from a third people called Saxons. From such coincidences he concluded that these were the original seats of his Jutes, Angles and Saxons[85].

---

84. *ibid.*, 72.
85. *On the Origin of the English*, by Elis Wadstein (Uppsala, 1927).

But it is now pretty evident that the main bulk of the continental element in the composition of the British provincials hailed from the Frisian shore between the Ems and the Rhine, who for centuries by infiltration had been entering the province from the Firth of Forth along the whole of the east and south coasts as far as Cornwall, occupying to a more or less extent each of the Britains under Roman rule and becoming, thereby, *Britanni* along with the rest of the population. They all spoke one and the same Frisian speech. They had no special name that we know of, but we have sure evidence that by the mid-sixth century they were calling themselves Angles and Frisians (to the Romans, of course, if they named them at all, they would have been mere *Saxones*), distinguishing between these two groups. By the end of the century the term Angles was current in papal letters as a denomination of all the English speaking-peoples in the island.

By Bede's time, the name of the Frisians in Britain had passed out of use (except sparsely in the Lowlands); certainly Bede betrays no remembrance of them or at least he does not mention them. By Bede's time too, the Angles and Frisians (of 554), all of them styled Angles by the end of that century, were now grouped under three names, Angles, Saxons, Jutes, whom Bede, working backwards from the known to the unknown, imagined and boldly declared to have been ' of three most powerful peoples of Germany', for had he not even found out exactly whence they came?

The map provides ample proof that the Angles of the territorium of Camulodunum (*Colchester*), that of Verulamium (*St. Albans*), that of Calleva Atrebatum (*Silchester*) and that of Noviomagus Regnensium (*Chichester*) took the name of Saxons (East, Middle, West, and South respectively)—not because they hailed from any ' Saxony' on the continent, but to distinguish themselves by this Roman appellation from their fellow-Angles, who occupied the territorium of Venta Icenorum (*Caistor by Norwich*) and that of Ratae Coritanorum (*Leicester*), who styled themselves East and Middle Angles respectively. It is true that Bede also enumerates among the Angles of Britain in his day, ' the Mercians, the whole stock of the Northumbrians, *i.e.* those who dwell to the north of the river Humber, and the rest of the peoples of the Angles', but whether these or some of them had not previously been known as Frisians is more than questionable.

The Jutes, being quite distinct from the Angles or Saxons, must have been those whom Procopius calls Frisians. As we have seen, they entered Kent from the Lowlands, under Octa. From the Jutes (says Bede)[86] are descended those who occupy Kent, the Isle of Wight,

---

86. *Historia ecclesiastica*. . . i., 15.

and those still called Jutes in 'Hampshire'. We find that those of Kent never called themselves Jutes, but preferred to be known as Cantware, which is simply *Cantiaci* translated into their speech. As for the Jutes of Wight and 'Hampshire' we have sure evidence that they were intruders in the canton of the Belgae (now known as Gewisse), who first arrived there in 514. It can also be shewn that they came from Kent[87].

The general conclusion is that all these Frisian-speaking folk and others of whatever origin, both from within and without the Roman Empire, entered into the composition of the *Britanni*, who on the Revolt of Maximus in 383 are found 'retaining the Roman name but not the law and custom', and who later were sending out appeals for Roman aid against the Picts and Scots, humbly apologizing for what evils they had done and for disparaging the Roman name as a term of contempt. And all these *Britanni*, the author of the *de excidio*, followed by Bede, mistook for Britons.

But there is more. Not only does the *de excidio* mistake these *Britanni* for Britons, but (again followed by Bede) ascribes their troubles and anxieties entirely to the raids of Picts and Scots, who were ever bearing down on leaderless and defenceless citizens. We know however, from other sources that the provincials of Britain at that time in common with the rest of the Roman world were being driven to desperation by Governmental oppression. For 'the vast bureaucratic machine of the later Roman empire was collapsing under its own weight and was drawing off the life-blood of its peoples in a taxation more crippling than any that modern men have experienced.' The very name of Roman citizen was being repudiated as almost abhorrent by the Romans themselves. Noblemen (like Vortigern) were driven to wish no longer to be Romans. They preferred to be barbarians. Barbaria was more acceptable than Romanitas, which explains its growing pressure. Barbaria was in the ascendant, till the strain was eased by Aëtius in 443, when south-east Britain was brought under the jurisdiction of the English.'

The origins of the English are to be found in the *Britanni* of the fifth century, liberated from Romanitas.

---

87. Bede (iii, 9) says that St. Birinus [A.D. 635] first entered the land of the Gewisse, but in the legendary life of St. Birinus, the saint is said to have tarried three days at the place where he landed, before he preached to the Gewisse " And among those who heard him in that place were many who had been previously converted to the Catholic Faith by the preaching of Blessed Augustine.' (Bright, *Early English Church History*, 169 ; Field's *St. Berin*, 62—3). This points to the Jutes and serves to indicate that they had arrived in Hampshire from Kent. In other words, they were not *de transmarinis partibus*, from abroad, as Bede would have it.

THE ANGLO-SAXON CHRONICLE.

Within twenty years from Bede's death in 735 one of the constituents of the Anglo-Saxon Chronicle (a highly composite document of Alfred's time) had been compiled. This particular constituent (from 449 to 754) originated in the newly-organized Kingdom of Wessex as so far consolidated by Ceadwalla and Ine (685—726). It consists (to begin with) of earlier annals dealing with Kent and Sussex, which are followed by similar early annals of the Gewisse of 'Wiltshire'; the Jutes of 'Hampshire' and Wight; and the West Saxons (originally and properly so called) of 'Berkshire'. All these earlier annals, welded together, were now 'touched-up' to make them accord with the 'picturesque writing' of Bede, in which the *Britanni* or provincials are assumed to have been all Britons, who were being invaded from the continent and driven back.

Thus, Hengist lands in Kent and conquers it in four victories over the Britons. Aelle lands in Sussex and conquers it in three victories over the Britons. 'Cerdic and Cynric, his son' land in 'Hampshire', winning four victories over the Britons. Stuf and Wihtgar also land in 'Hampshire' and win a victory over the Britons. Ceawlin the West Saxon wins three astounding victories over the Britons. And so the story proceeds in one undeviating series of victories over the Britons, so that sober inquirers have been tempted not only to doubt these statements but even to throw them entirely aside as hopeless. J. M. Kemble in 1849 was driven to the conclusion that they were devoid of historical truth in every detail. The annals, however, are by no means incredible, provided the underlying flaw on which they are based is recognised and that they are stripped of every reference to continental invaders and retreating Britons, which have been naively foisted into them in the wake of Bede's glowing narrative and ' picturesque writing ', actuated as it is by untempered patriotism and anti-British animus.

Moreover, in the Wessex portion of these annals down to 754, in which one detects a purposeful assemblage of three separate sets of earlier annals, to wit, those of the Gewisse from Cerdic, those of the Jutes from Stuf and Wihtgar, and those of the West Saxons properly so called from Ceawlin, one may likewise detect the evident intention of the compilers, which was to tone down the differences between these three peoples, Gewisse, Jutes, and West Saxons, so as to further the cause of their unification into the single state of the 'new Wessex', which had been begun by Ceadwalla and strengthened by Ine.

To this very laudable end we note illaudible means, whereby the names of the Gewisse and of the Jutes are never allowed to appear, both of them being palmed off as West Saxons ; whereby also Cerdic and Cynric, leaders of the Gewisse, Stuf, Wihtgar, etc, leaders of the Jutes, are represented as genuine West Saxons; whereby too all conflicts between Gewisse, Jutes, and West Saxons are not only minimized to the last degree, but (a more serious indictment) even transmuted into struggles between West Saxons and impossible Britons to the repeated, never varying discomfiture of the latter. In brief, the West Saxon annalists for a desirable political end are found not to be averse to disguising and to distorting the truth. One may also add that they not only suppress the names of the Gewisse and Jutes in the composition of the 'new Wessex', but also completely ignore a third element, viz., the Britons of 'Somerset', who actually retained their own princes (as at Glastonbury) down to the tenth century[88].

From the confused welter of these West Saxon annals, the story of the two Jutish gangs, who landed in 'Hampshire' as told in the *de excidio*, may easily be distinguished. By their treatment of this incident light is thrown on the mental approach of the annalists. For whereas the *de excidio* opens out a wide view of the history of these Jutes, who for exactly one hundred and fifty years (514—664) ceased not to war against their neighbours, no indication is given of this in the annals. Nor is there any mention of the great battle, in which the Jutes were finally brought to a stand and ultimately 'merged in the West Saxon crown', which battle was the celebrated Siege of the Badonic Hill, fought in 665, and won over the Jutes, doubtless by Cenwalh, king of the Gewisse. So it may well be (even as Guest opined) that Badbury Rings in Dorset was its site.

NENNIUS.

The compilation known as Nennius's *History of the Britons*[89] dates from A.D. 829, though there may have been an earlier edition.

It consists for the most part of 'excerpts' drawn from older sources, Roman, Irish, English and British, which the compiler, bewildered by the *de excidio* as distorted by Bede, has done his best to harmonize with the same, for which reason he has even incorporated tales told by Welsh *cyfarwyddiaid*, professional story-tellers. Such harmonization, however, being impossible if true history was to be conveyed, the value of his work lies precisely where he fails to achieve it and where in consequence he has willy-nilly preserved historical data older than either Bede or the *de excidio*, however much contaminated by them.

88. Harl. Ped. xxv. (*Nennius* p. 111.).
89. *Chronica Minora* iii, 143—219. For translations see *Six Old English Chronicles*, 383—416; J. O. Jones, *O Lygad y Ffynnon*, pp. 209—246; *Nennius* (S.P.C.K.), pp. 35—84, 114—121.

The difficulties against which Nennius had to contend are plain, for he tells us that he was a disciple of Elfoddw, bishop in Gwynedd, who in 768 had brought the Britons of Wales into agreement with the Anglo-Saxons on the hotly-disputed matter of dating Easter. This was subsequent to the publication by Bede in 731 of Pope Gregory's Letter, from which it was made quite clear to the Britons that Canterbury (apart from Augustine personally) had no jurisdiction over Welsh Christians. Thus Nennius had become familiar not only with the novel notions let loose by the *de excidio* as interpreted by Bede, but also with their very ready acceptance by Anglo-Saxon scholars and patriots in the wake of Bede. His problem was how to reconcile this new and prevailing fashion of recording Anglo-Saxon history with his awkward ' excerpts ' or historical memoranda, some of which were evidently older than the *de excidio*, although Nennius may not have realized it. He tells us plainly in his Preface that the learned men of his day had shirked the task, although many had tried. So oppressed was he by British *hebitudo* that he was driven to attempt the work himself, admitting in his humility that he was only like a chattering jay. Thus, in a more or less garbled form, he conveyed to posterity precious bits of information, which otherwise would certainly have perished ; for (as Lappenberg suggests)[90] the very excellence of Bede's History may well have proved fatal to the survival of much earlier historical material. Anglo-Saxon history of a decidedly propagandist and aggressive sort (as illustrated in the Wessex annals) was in the ascendant, which proved all but too strong for Nennius as it has proved altogether too strong for many a British inquirer since. No wonder then that his reputation as a historian has fluctuated from age to age. His work fell on evil days. Not a single complete copy of it survives. His very name all but disappeared, whilst (thanks to Bede) the Auctor Badonicus of the *de excidio* under the name of Gildas, identified with Gildas Albanius, was acclaimed on all sides as the historiographus of the Britons.

Nennius devotes eighteen chapters (31 to 49) to the career of Vortigern, whom Bede by inference had magnified into King of the Britons and lord of all southern Britain. These chapters include : (1) a valuable genealogy of Vortigern (49) going back into the fourth century and continued down to A. D. 829 with sundry particulars as to Vortigern's sons (48) ; (2) four extracts (32—35, 39, 47) taken by Rhun, son of Urien in the early seventh century from a lost ' Book of the blessed Germanus', wherein Vortigern appears with no reference of any kind to Saxons ; (3) deductions (36) from Bede's paraphrase of the *de excidio* ; and (4) several distinct stories or romances (37—38, 40—46), *cyfarwyddiadau*, told by professional story-tellers (in the manner of the Four Branches of the *Mabinogi* and similar

---

90. Lappenberg, i, xxxv.

tales), which last in particular serve to bring the book into line with Bede's disastrous mishandling of the story of the 'Saxon advent' as told in the *de excidio*.

The *cyfarwydd* or story-teller speaks merely to entertain, as often as not with his tongue in his cheek. The stories, as given here by Nennius, are all formed upon that of Hengist and Horsa, Bede's report of the same being the material on which he is working, into which fortunately he also works other and independent material including what he knew of the 'transit' of Octa from the Lowlands of Scotland into Kent. Thus he makes Hengist say to Vortigern (38) —

> ' I will invite my son with his cousin, for they are warlike men, to fight against the Scots. And you give them the districts which are in the North, by the Wall, which is called Gwawl.' And [Vortigern] commanded him to invite them. And [Hengist] invited Octha and Ebissa with forty keels. And these, when they sailed round the Picts, wasted the Orkney Islands, and came and occupied very many districts beyond the Frisian Sea even to the border of the Picts.

The story-teller naturally made his audience to understand that Octa and Ebissa started from the continent in their forty keels, circumnavigating the Picts from east to west, for it was to watch the Scots, *i.e.*, the Irish, over against N.W. Ireland that they were directed. On their way they wasted the Orkneys, terrifying all Pictland, and then establishing themselves in the western Lowlands opposite Ireland to keep an eye on the Scots—not far from the Roman wall beyond the Frisian Sea. By the Frisian Sea, therefore, must be understood the Solway Firth or at least that part of it, into which the river Nith flows, on the banks of which stands Dumfries, ' the Fort of the Frisians'. As there was a *Litus Fresicum*[91] 'Frisian Shore ' along the Firth of Forth, ' the very many districts beyond the Frisian Sea up to the border of the Picts ' lay in the Lowlands between the two Firths of Solway and Forth, and doubtless it was from this Frisian Shore along the Forth that the fleet of Octa and Ebissa started.

In brief, Octa and Ebissa, when detached from Bede's story of Hengist and Horsa, into which the British *cyfarwydd* has worked their history, appear as Lowlanders of the mid-fifth century, Frisian or Jutish leaders in the Roman service, commissioned like Arthur to protect the province not against invading Saxons but against

---
91. Jocelyn's *Kentigern*, c. 8.

plundering Picts and Scots. One may safely ascribe the contemporaneous appearance of Arthur and Octa at this time to arrangements directed by Aëtius as a consequence of the Letter of Appeal sent to him in 446[92].

An old list of Arthur's twelve victories is given, which in the setting provided for them by Nennius would appear to have been fought against the Saxons and even against Octa (although Saxons are not named), the Siege of the Badonic Hill also being deliberately foisted into the series from the *de excidio* as interpreted by Bede, to buttress the notion. Not one of the sites of these battles has been satisfactorily identified, but doubtless they should be sought to the North and West rather than to the East.

The *ordo* or council of the Romano-British city of Durovernum Cantiacorum (*Canterbury*) was still functioning when Octa ' passed over ' into Kent, but if he occupied the old extinct office of ' Count of the Saxon Shore', he would naturally have laid claim to all its forts from Branodunum (*Brancaster*, in Norfolk) to Portus Adurni (*Porchester*) in Sussex. His advent however was not welcomed by the Cantiaci for we have sure evidence of four battles, through which Kent became Frisian or Jutish. As it was at this time that ' kings were being annointed', denoting the decline and fall of city rule, the fact that Oeric Oisc, the son of Octa, became the first king of Kent indicates the final and permanent supremacy of the Frisians or Jutes in this quarter.

The Cantiacan opposition fell back on the territorium of London, whilst in the adjoining canton of Noviomagus Regnensium (*Chichester*) which still survives under the name of Sussex, rose another king Aelle by name, who would seem to have headed a widely-spread resistance to the Frisians or Jutes, for we find him raised to the position of Bretwalda, i.e., *gwledig* or supreme ruler over all the English south of the Humber. It may very well be that this was in consequence of his capture of the Roman fort of Anderida in 491 (not of course from impossible Britons as stated in the Chronicle) but from Oeric Oisc, who claimed it as successor to his father, Octa.

Notwithstanding this defeat of the Jutes, and their forced acceptance of Aelle as Bretwalda, their aggressive ardour did not cease, because (1) a considerable interval elapsed after Aelle's death before the rise of a second Bretwalda, during which time the Jutes renewed their strength ; and (2) in 514 they landed in the canton of Venta Belgarum (*Winchester*), where, after having

---

92. It would appear that Bede's story of Hengist and Horsa is but a debased version of the credible account of Octa and Ebissa. Hengist and Horsa are really nicknames, ' Stallion ' and ' Mare,' standing for Octa and Ebissa respectively.

received an accession to their forces, they swept over the cantou from sea to sea, as far as the Bristol Channel, effecting great destruction, and took possession of 'Hampshire' and the Isle of Wight. As we have seen, this is the historic event, which the author of the *de excidio* treated as the first coming of the English into Britain.

MERFYN (825—844), RHODRI THE GREAT (844—877).

The advent of Merfyn Frych, the Manxman, in whose reign Nennius dates his book, inaugurated a new forceful period in Welsh history, extending to the days of Howel Dda (*d.*950) and Morgan Hen (*d.*974), the eponym of Morgannwg. Merfyn became King of Gwynedd in 825, and judging from the description of him as Camwri[93], his reign may be regarded as either that of an oppressor or as one of great glory, or both. He was of high birth, descended from the ruling line of Gwynedd up to Cunedda Wledig, from the rulers of the Isle of Man up to Maxim Wletic, and also from Coel Odebog of Aeron 'Ayr' in the western Lowlands through Llywarch Hen, the cousin of Urien Rheged. His court was known as a rendezvous of learned men, and an Irish writer is much concerned lest some of his brethren 'might be made to blush in the presence of Merfyn, the glorious King of the Britons'[94]. In England, too, his name was known, his seat at 'Cair Segeint' in Arfon being called 'Merfyn's town'. By his marriage to Nest, sister of Cyngen, the last king of Powys of the old line, their son Rhodri, surnamed 'the Great', succeeded to the realm of Powys in addition to that of Gwynedd. The name 'Cymry' for the Britons of Wales seems to have expanded under the rule of these two kings.

Nennius's 'History of the Britons' marks Merfyn's reign, whilst much Welsh poetry is attributable to this period, mostly from the Powysian borders. It deals mainly with heroic characters of earlier times such as the northerners Llywarch Hen and Urien Rheged, and those of an old Powysian line, which hailed from Llystin Wynnan in Caereinion, such as Cynddylan and his sister Heledd. A sad note runs through this poetry, for which reason historians have been tempted to hear in it the melancholy cry of the Welsh Britons, ever in full retreat, and thus to find justification for their assumptions, besides giving strong support to our egregious Celtomaniacs. It was but yesterday that Ceawlin, King of the West Saxons (560—593), was believed to have penetrated from the Thames valley right up to the borders of Chester with fire and sword. Wroxeter was made to have gone up in flames, and this Powysian poetry was quoted as singing piteously 'the death-song of Uriconium'— 'the white town in the valley, the hall of its chieftain left without

---
93. *Ancient Laws of Wales*, i. 342.
94. Gougaud, *Christianity in Celtic Lands*, 252—3.

fire, without light, without songs, the silence broken only by the eagle's scream, the eagle which had swallowed fresh drink, heart's blood of Kynddylan the fair'. Bede himself could not have done better.

Our Powysian poetry, however, tells a different story. Offa King of Mercia (757—796) had built a rampart ' from sea to sea', marking the old line of division between the Britons of Wales and the *Britanni* of the east. It stretched from Prestatyn in Flintshire as far as Bridge Sollars in Herefordshire, from which place the R. Wye served as boundary till it flows into the Severn. Thus, the old territorium of Deva (Chester), taking in the whole estuary of the R. Dee, and the old canton of Viriconium Cornoviorum (*Wroxeter*) on either side of the Severn were marked off as being outside the jurisdiction of the Britons, which jurisdicton was well to the west of the Roman road from Magnae (*Kenchester*) to Chester. Offa, as King of Mercia, was certainly justified in fixing the rampart as he did, and he may well have allowed the Britons, more than they were entitled to.

But in this Powysian poetry we find ample evidence that the Britons had been encroaching, forcing themselves into places like Baschurch and even as far east as the Ercals on either side of the R. Tern. We may sorrow with the poet weeping over ' Eglwysseu Bassa',[95] but when we realize that these were in Mercian territory, named after a Mercian Prince, Bassa, who doubtless owned them as lawfully as St. David owned the many churches called by his name, it may (if possible) assuage the melancholy, the ' Celtic melancholy ', instilled into us by pseudo-history. Be of good cheer. A map of modern Wales does not lie, when it reveals plainly that the Welshman has not fared so badly both in preserving his own legitimate ground (which Maxim Wletic left in his charge) and even in extending it.

ASSER.

On the death of Gwgon, king of Ceredigion in 871, Rhodri, son of Merfyn, added to his realm the land of Seisyllwg, which comprised the four cantrevs of Ceredigion together with the three of Ystrad Tywi ; so that in addition to the whole of Gwynedd and Powys, his rule now extended right across South Wales from Aberdovey to Swansea. That same year Alfred the Great, king of Wessex, came to power, whilst shortly after Asser is reported as living in South Wales at St. David's, who in 884 was invited to Alfred's court to live there part-time at the king's service. There survives

---

95. *Arch. Camb.* (1944.) pp. 145—6.

a famous book attributed to Asser on the Life of Alfred,[96] of which and from which we have yet very much to learn, and without it much might have still proved doubtful.

Thus, we gather among other things that at that time Wales was known as Britannia (as first brought forward by Gweirydd ap Rhys)[97] and its inhabitants as Britons (with no mention of Cymry); that the West Saxons were all of them by the Britons called *Geguuis*, i.e., Gew-wys, the Gewisse, which is no small check on what Bede says; that Alfred on his mother's side was a Jute ' of the seed of Stuf and Wihtgar', Jutes, *i.e.*, those who were ' admitted into the island' in 514, which corrects the impression left by the Anglo-Saxon Chronicle, that it was Offa who built the ' great rampart between Britannia (*i.e.*, Wales) and Mercia from sea to sea', which is the first known mention of Offa's Dyke. We also learn that the six sons of Rhodri Mawr succeeded their father in the rule of all Wales outside the following ancient kingdoms in the south :—

Dyfed, whose ruler was Hyfaidd.
Brycheiniog, under Helised son of Teudubr.
Glywysing, under Howel, son of Rhys.
Gwent, under Brochfael and Ffernfael, sons of Meurig.

And even more important, we are assured that all these kings of Wales sided with Alfred in his great stand against the Scandinavian hordes who would reduce Britain under pagan sway.

ARMES PRYDAIN.

But unfortunately there were men in Wales who had other thoughts, attributable to the falsification of history.

A poem, ' the Prophecy of Britain', appears sometime in this period, consisting of 199 lines as arranged by Skene, possibly (as may hereafter be discovered) dating itself. The inhabitants of Wales were by this date recognizable as Cymry, by which name the poet calls them fourteen times (with Kymro ' Welshman ' once) distinguishing them most carefully from the Cornish and the Bretons, and even from the Strathclyde Welsh and also the ' Men of the North'. His aim is to multiply the sorts of people, who will combine, aided too by other folks, Irish, Danish, Manx, Pictish. It would seem as though he had been reading Nennius or at least had heard the tales, for he refers to Hengist and Horsa, to Vortigern and Vortimer,

---

96. Asser, *Life of King Alfred* edited by Stevenson. Translations—Giles *Six Old English Chronicles*, 43—86; J. O. Jones *O Lygad y Ffynnon*, 251—302; L. C. Jane *Asser's Life of King Alfred* (1908).
97. *Hanes*, i., 12.

to what happened at Thanet, etc. Obviously to him the Cymry
were the folk driven out of England into Wales. The Gewisse and all
the English were, (not the *Britanni* of the fifth century, but trans-
marine foreigners—in fact the hordes of Jutes, Angles and Saxons,
who according to Bede had sailed across from Denmark, etc. His
policy (if we may call it a policy) was nothing less than this. The
Cymry were to rise as one man to drive the Gewisse and the English
in general, bag and baggage, out of Britain. Outside peoples would
join them, Cadwaladr and Cynan would be their leaders, of whom
he seems to know more than we do, whilst Dewi Sant would assist
from the heavenly places.

The poem is written with great vigour. It reveals how the shadow
of Bede had fallen on Wales and how falsified history may beguile
a people.

HOWEL DDA (*d*.950) AND BLEGYWRYD.

The sane policy, adopted by all the kings of Wales and backed by
Bishop Asser, in supporting Alfred the Great against the Scandinavian
invaders, was continued by their successors, of whom the most
distinguished was Howel, son of Cadell, son of Rhodri Mawr.
That policy was in the line of true history, being essentially the same
as that pursued by Roman Britain in the mid-fifth century, when
Arthur and Octa were commissioned to repel the Picts and Scots
since which time there had occurred no such invasions till these
of the Scandinavians in the ninth century.

But what of Wales itself? We have seen that, when the Western
Empire in its collapse in the fifth century had everywhere disintegrated,
Roman Britain too had fallen asunder into fragments, which in their
turn fell into smaller pieces. Wales, as left in 383 by Maxim Wletic,
had become a country of small principalities. But by the time
of Howel the tide of disintegration had long since turned here as
elsewhere. Wherever feasible, the fragments were coalescing. And
the mind of Wales was confronted with a momentous choice as
to how to achieve that unification of its Britons, of which men
were dreaming, whether by violence which seemed to many an
obvious way or by suasion based on Christian culture.

Howel and his supporters adopted the latter course. As testified
by universal tradition, he undertook the codification of Welsh law
and custom. He would bring all the Cymry under one body of rules.
which should prevail throughout the length and breadth of the land.
His chief adviser was Blegywryd ab Einon of Gwent, a man of great
learning and experience in the law. Both of Howel and of Blegywryd
we know very little, but as early as the first half of the twelfth century
they were remembered by a grateful people, the former as Howel

Dda 'the Good,' and the latter as 'that most famous man'[98]. The impression left by these two on the Cymry was deep and lasting and salutary.

MORGAN HEN (d. 974).

The realm of Morgannwg, which took its name from Morgan the Aged and which at one time stretched from the Wye to the Tawe, comprising in part the old principalities of Glywysing and Erging and the whole of Gwent, differs from all the kingdoms of ancient Wales in this respect, that it included the Romano-British territoria of Ariconium (*Weston under Penyard*) and of Venta Silurum (*Caerwent*) together with the Roman fortress of Isca (*Caerleon*), to say nothing of Cardiff. Doubtless, this has proved a prime cause of a felt distinction between this portion of Wales and the rest.

VNBEINYAETH PRYDAIN.

I have submitted that the term ' Cymry ' as a national appellation may have originated in the North and entered Wales with Cunedda Wledig about A.D. 400. But not till the ninth century do we find sure evidence that it was prevailing in Wales, and to what extent is doubtful. It may be that one will have to associate the presumably growing popularity of the name with a remarkable passage found in the earliest known copies of the Laws of Howel, which states that the Bard of the Household is to sing ' Vnbeinyaeth Prydain ' before the host in the day of battle and fighting[99]. The words mean *monarchia Britanniae*, the monarchy of Britain, which words actually appear on the so-called Pillar of Eliseg[100], of the ninth century, in some association with Maximus. If, as suggested, they mean the monarchy of Wales (where Prydain equates with Britannia and this with Wales), the song points to the idea of Cymric unity.

GRUFFUDD AP LLYWELYN (1039—1063).

There now followed decades of confusion, for which (as far as I know) no adequate explanation has ever been submitted.

We may well believe that the Britons of Wales under the designation of Cymry, 'compatriots', were at this time becoming steadily conscious of themselves as one people and one land—*Kambri, Kambria*. We may also believe that age-long loyalties to their small but ancient principalities[101] were very strong, for the Welsh

---

98. *Book of Llan Dâv*, 241 'Hiuel da f. Cattell.' 219 'famosissimus ille vir Bledcuirit filius Eniaun.'
99. *Welsh Medieval Law* (A. W. Wade-Evans), 22, 167, 349—50; *Ancient Laws of Wales*, ii, 763, 830.
100. Nennius, p. 33.
101. *gwlad, gwladoedd*. (*Welsh Medieval Law*, 342—3.).

were conservative, even to a fault, even to *hebitudo*, an old failing of theirs. They were thus torn between fidelity to the old arrangement as left in the fifth century and the prospect and dream of '*Kambria*,' *Cymry yn y therfyn, Cymry benbaladr*.[102] All this is true, but hardly sufficient to account for the cross-purposes at work in the period which followed the death of Howel Dda.

Let us take a glance back. Who were the Britons of Wales? Historically, they were in the main the descendants of two hill-tribes of Roman times, who had been left outside the cantonal arrangement of that portion of Roman Britain to the east of them. These were the Ordovices and the Demetae. [I here omit the Deceangli of ' Flintshire ' who were presumably in whole or in part within the territorium of Deva (Chester) and also the Silures, who were organized into a canton with a ' capital ' at Venta Silurum (Caerwent). For it was to the west of these that the ' Britons ' as distinct from the *Britanni* of the east lay, whom Maxim Wletic left to guard the land.] These western folk we must account as the *nuclei* from whom and about whom the Cymry have sprung, taking in later the Deceangei and the Silures.

From these small beginnings they had improved and strengthened their position. We find them conscious of their Roman connection, symbolized for them by mythical ancestors, Brutus the Roman consul and Britto of the stock of Troy, and by the known descent of their rulers from Roman generals, especially Maxim Wletic. They were a Christian people devoted to the Church as inherited by them from Roman Britain and Gaul and as testified by their many noble monasteries and daughter establishments, whose founders they held in highest regard, as testified, too, by the long and successful stand which they made against the pretension of Canterbury. They were a cultured people as evidenced by their poetry, by the works of their professional story-tellers, by Nennius's gallant attempt, in the face of overwhelming difficulties, to preserve the truth of their historic origins, and by the codification of their laws and customs, wherein it is plain that master hands have been at work. They were ' strong in arms,' for they kept the country committed to their care by Maxim Wletic and even enlarged its borders.

All this and more is true. But they had received what may be called a psychological set-back, a blow all the more tragic because it affected the mind of Wales. Their historical memories, clear and simple in all conscience, had been challenged by the plausible speculations of the Venerable Bede, the greatest historian of the age, who hated them and all their works. I am persuaded that this was the most disconcerting trial ever endured by the Cymry, which affects them through the schools to this day. Not that the mass of them

---

102. *Welsh Medieval Law*, 1.

had ever heard of Bede or his speculations, though the tales of Hengist and Hors had spread as evidenced by Nennius and *Armes Prydain*. Nor do I refer to the activities of scholars, who were evidently too stupid to preserve valuable memoranda of history such as those partly rescued for us by Nennius. Perhaps, not one or two in a generation ever read Bede. But those who did or to whom his ideas descended, a thoughtful and anxious few such as are found in every age, must have had their whole conception of Welsh history upturned with depressing effect, which conveyed to others, spread throughout all ranks. Ridiculous as these ideas were, they amounted to no less than this, that the Britons of Wales were the *Britanni* of England displaced.

In virtue of this doctrine, which I cannot describe as other than monstrous, the Cymry had come to suspect that they were a losing people[103] although the reverse was the truth. They were well on the high road to becoming a nation.

Consider the effect that a suspicion of this kind would have upon a spirited people. Their grip on what they held would tighten. Fear of change with aversion to political experiments would follow. And such would seem to have been their mental outlook at this time. They swung between two opinions, pressed hard as they were along their borders, whether to cling tightly to their traditional principalities or to follow some bold war-leader towards the attractive goal of political unity.

At first, kings in the legitimate line of their descent strove to bring all Wales under the rule of their particular families, which roused resentment and stubborn opposition on the part of rival families. This continued for some half a century with no lasting success. But as the sense of Welsh unity did not abate but rather

---

103. The Reverend Thomas Price, 'Carnhuanawc,' Welsh historian after writing 367 pages of his *Hanes Cymru* (1842), is reduced to sum up as follows :—

'In the course of the preceding history it has been seen that the Welsh nation was falling into decay from age to age, that her territories were being narrowed, and her branching tribes, into which she was divided, were undergoing complete extinction, until at last there was nought left to the larger British community in this island except the remnant people and the fragment of land which is comprised within the borders of *Wales*.'

However the gallant old patriot is not behind hand to balance this tale of woe as well as he may, which he does as follows :—

'But here Providence saw well to check the destruction, and for more than a thousand years, although many an unfortunate circumstance befell our nation, yet their name was not put out and their numbers were not diminished. And inasmuch as this was the judgement for our iniquities, to wit, such territorial diminution, yet I perceive great cause for thankfulness for mercy bestowed upon us even in the midst of correction, as I know not on the face of the earth of a region more beautiful, more blissful, and all in all more desirable than the land of *Wales*.'

grew, there emerged war leaders of doubtful origin, bent on accomplishing what the others had failed to effect. The last and most conspicuous of these was Gruffudd ap Llywelyn, who, gaining power in North Wales at the expense of legitimate rulers, won a sudden and startling victory over the English at Rhydygroes[104] on the Severn. This may well have stirred enthusiasm among the Britons at large and reconciled them to his overlordship, had he diverted and confined his efforts to withstanding border aggressions. But as Gweirydd ap Rhys[105] insists, he was but a usurper even in North Wales to say nothing of the South. Immediately after his victory at Rhydygroes he proceeds to devastate Seisyllwg, including the church lands of Llanbadarn Fawr, to defeat its lawful ruler in a battle and to abduct his wife. His evident intention, doubtless, was to unite all Wales under a sole ruler as well as to restore the ancient borders of Wales eastwards.[106] He actually became King of all Wales for a brief period, leaving the remembrance of such a *fait accompli* to become a foretaste of what might some day prove permanently possible. He certainly gave an impetus to the idea of Welsh unity. But when he had attained the height of his ambition, and the hour had come for England to settle terms with him, Wales rapidly reverted to the conditions of her traditional order, and Gruffudd ap Llywelyn met death at the hands of his own men.

The obstacles in the way of the unity of Wales were such as no bare coercion could overcome. The task required, then as now, spiritual weapons, of which Wales being a Christian land, was not ignorant. Even with her history bedevilled, Wales, true to evangelical principles, may well have realized the goal of her desire, as far as was consistent in the Christian scheme.

A. W. WADE-EVANS.

---

104. The victory at Rhydygroes (Buttington Bridge) reminded som reader of Nennius (or at least of Nennius material) of the legendary Battle of Mount Badon, in which Arthur was imagined to have effected wonders over Saxons. Mount Badon was even located at the Black Bank near by (to which notion doubtless the name '*Botinton*' lent support) by the author of the late mediaeval tale 'Rhonabwy's Dream.'

105. *Hanes* i. 455 " trawsfeddiannwr oedd efe hyd yn oed o Wynedd, heb sôn am y Deheubarth."

106. *Hanes*, i., 453, ' i'w hen derfynau, y cytunasai'r Saeson a'r Cymry er ys oesoedd cyn hyn yn eu cylch.' Here Gweirydd ap Rhys displays true historical instinct, that the borders between the Britons and their fellow-*Britanni* of the east had been determined upon of old.

THE AGE OF THE PRINCES.*

WHATEVER the difference in opinion on the character of Tudor policy in Wales, the Act of Union of 1536, it must be recognized, brought to a close the period of independent growth for Welsh political and legal institutions. National consciousness henceforth developed in isolation from the mechanism of the *state*, finding ultimate expression in institutions of a non-political kind. But was it the inevitable fate of Wales to become a stateless nation ? In answer to that question it can at least be said that all the potentialities of normal political growth were present in mediæval Wales. In this lecture I propose to examine some of those potentialities, and to indicate the direction given to them by the thirteenth century princes of Gwynedd.

Most of you, it can be assumed, are familiar with Gerald's classic description of social and political conditions in Wales at the close of the twelfth century. You will recall the following observations about the habits of his fellow-countrymen. " They do not concern themselves with trade, shipping or manufactures, or with hardly any other occupation except training for war . . . . Nearly everyone lives on the produce of animals, oats, milk, cheese and butter, eating meat in large quantities and consuming bread rather sparingly." This is no doubt a reasonably accurate commentary. The prevalence of pastoral conditions and the economic self-sufficiency of the Welsh country-side were visible features which could not have deceived so intelligent an observer as Gerald. He has also given us a true enough picture of the political state of Wales with its local particularism and continuous civil strife. Yet it is by no means the whole picture. Gerald, for example, never refers to the old native laws of Wales which were even in his life-time taking on a new lease of life, alleviating to some extent the anarchy which fills the background of his picture. Indeed, in less than a century following Gerald's death we meet with a very different set of conditions. It is a matter for regret that so many still labour under the false impression that Welsh native society continued more or less static from the time of Gerald down to the eve of the Edwardian settlement. The fact is that during the intervening period tremendous changes were taking place in many directions ; and if we are to grasp the significance of the political changes sponsored by the princes of Gwynedd, it is necessary in the first place to attempt an explanation of the changes at work in the social and legal system of Wales during the century which lies roughly between the date of Gerald's tour (1188) and the fall of Llywelyn II in 1282. Our main source of information will be the ancient laws of Wales—commonly known as the *Law of Hywel Dda.*

---
* This lecture was first delivered at the University College of North Wales, Bangor, in January, 1945.

It should be realized at the outset that the surviving texts of the Welsh laws are not official promulgations, but consist rather of a series of text-books compiled during the later part of the Middle Ages. They are the work of experienced teachers of law, writing at different periods for students and practitioners. The principal aim of these teachers, moreover, was to give instruction in the history of the legal system, since contemporary legal usages were ultimately based on older practices. One of them observes in the preamble to his work that he has compiled his book from the best works " I have discovered in Gwynedd, Powys and Deheubarth . . . . and whosoever would wish to become a magistrate, he must know the contents of this book so that he may be worthy of that office." Yet it can be shown that large sections of Iorwerth ap Madoc's text were already, at the time he wrote, part of the antiquities of law. This is also a feature of many of the other texts. The living jurisprudence of the thirteenth century (and much of this was an intermediate growth subsequent to the age of Hywel Dda) is introduced incidentally into the text, by way of commentary as a rule on customs and practices which had long since ceased to operate, or which at least had been so much transformed as to be almost unrecognizable in their original guise. But there was good reason for this inclusion of the archaic. In the older portions of the law were embedded the precedents which enabled the lawyers to unravel the complexities of law. The point I am trying to make is well illustrated in the law relating to *galanas*—one of the basic institutions of mediaeval Wales.

One of the major problems of early society was the control of lawlessness and bloodshed arising out of family feuds following acts of homicide. Quite early in the history of primitive communities there can be perceived an organized effort to substitute for the blood-feud which normally followed fatal acts of violence, a compensatory payment in kind by the murderer's kindred to the kindred of the victim. In Wales the word *galanas* was originally used to describe both the act of killing and the subsequent blood-feud. Later on it came to denote the actual compensation paid to the victim's kindred, and in this sense *galanas* is the exact equivalent of the Teutonic *wergild*. Now this concept of *galanas* dominates the older portions of all the codal texts. They describe in detail how *galanas* is to be exacted from the murderer's paternal and maternal relatives as far as the ninth degree. Conversely, *galanas* was shared among the victim's kindred to the ninth degree. These rules, it is important to observe, were reproduced in detail throughout successive editions of the codes from the close of the twelfth century to the sixteenth century, although the old form of *galanas* payment had virtually disappeared by the beginning of the period with which this lecture is concerned. What accounts for the prominence given by the lawyers to this aspect of a system which had already lost much of its original validity?

By the year 1200, the old concept of *galanas*, it is known, had been replaced by an entirely different attitude towards crime, serious homicide being then punished by death and total confiscation of property at the hands of the *state*. The lawyers were now able to distinguish between crime and what we should call civil injury—between *cyflafan* (felony) and *cam* or *anghyfraith* (wrong or unlawful act); and a number of offences were being classified as crimes against society. As far as homicide was concerned, the laws make it clear that a period of transition preceded the emergence of a distinctly criminal jurisprudence. A phase of development can be observed in which *galanas* was still exacted, but in which ultimate responsibility for its payment rested upon the individual and not the *cenedl*—i.e., the family group to the ninth degree. It is also evident that it was not always an easy matter for the culprit to collect sufficient *galanas* to enable him to escape the extreme penalty of the law. The requirements of the old law, it would appear, were imposing a considerable strain on the tie of kindred. It is, indeed, impossible to study the provisions of the law relating to *galanas* without being struck by the evident reluctance of the culprit's kinsmen to co-operate voluntarily in the operation of the law. One feels that a spontaneous popular recoil from the rigid *galanas* system of the days of Hywel had been more responsible for the change which had occurred by the end of the twelfth century than any direct intervention by the *state*. I shall venture to add that the *state* itself, in handling this problem, was influenced more by impatience with obstacles to the smooth working of the old system than it was by the example of the Canon and Common Laws, although both the latter, no doubt, played some part in bringing about the change observed. On the other hand, if the older *galanas* system was disintegrating long before the accession of Llywelyn the Great, the underlying principles of that system survived into the thirteenth century, and were adapted to a new social background.

In cases of accidental homicide, for example, an action of *galanas* could be brought against the culprit by the nearest kinsfolk of the victim. But if *rhaith* (compurgation) went against him, the defendant was now obliged to bear the full burden of the *galanas* payment; and if he was unable to discharge the obligation, his share of the family lands passed as blood-land into the hands of the plaintiffs. In time, moreover, only the closest relative of the victim could demand damages. Henceforth, the *cenedl*—i.e., the circle of kindred to the ninth degree—had no function to perform in *galanas* actions. They were, in effect, ordinary civil actions between individual parties, and this action continued to be available where Welsh law was practised until the second half of the fifteenth century. But if, by the thirteenth century, kindred had ceased to have a technichal role in the working law of *galanas*, why did the lawyers (and here I return to my original question) take so much trouble to keep alive a knowledge of the early practice of *galanas* with all its detailed genealogical ramifications ? The answer is simply this. It is probable that many of the personal actions of Welsh law, such as contract and suretyship, were evolved after the time of Hywel; and the *cenedl* —i.e., the *galanas* kindred—was used to facilitate the procedure devised for these new actions. In actions of contract or suretyship, for example, where the defence was a denial of obligation, the law provided that the defendant should take a public oath to that effect supported by the oaths of six of his kindred—four to be paternal relatives and two maternal. The *rhaith* (oath-helpers) had to be selected from among those who would have paid *galanas* with the defendant. Those are the words which appear in a portion of the law which, I imagine, was very much alive in the thirteenth century, and in which there is no other reference to *galanas* except in a similar context. Since the *cenedl* or *galanas* groups also played an important part in the later law of real property (*cyfraith tir a daear*), it will be realised why the lawyers took such pains to describe in detail the traditional *galanas* law of Wales.

At the beginning of this period, therefore, the *cenedl*, the unit which was once responsible for the payment and receipt of *galanas*, in a large measure still dominated Welsh social and legal arrangements. It should perhaps be explained, in parenthesis, that the word *cenedl* bore other meanings ; and that shortly after the year 1200, this term (which in modern Welsh signifies a nation) was tending to be replaced, it would appear, by other words used to distinguish various aspects of the old institution of *cenedl*, such as *llwyth* for the *cenedl* as tribe, or *gwelygordd* for the *cenedl* as clan. But in its restricted sense, to which attention has been confined hitherto, the *cenedl* or *galanas* group to the ninth degree of affinity was not a rigid or coherent institution as were the tribe and clan. The late T. P. Ellis proved this beyond question. There existed an infinite overlapping of relationships so that only brothers and sisters could possibly belong to identical *galanas* circles. The institution of *cenedl* in this narrower sense was of no importance as far as public law (in the thirteenth century) was concerned. Its survival was ensured in order to facilitate the working an expanding private law administered under the eye of a *state* which was becoming increasingly powerful. This loose and fluid system of kinship offered no resistance to the growth of the *state* in Wales during the age of the two Llywelyns. This was not wholly the case with the system of *cenedl* in its broader aspects, i.e. as a tribal system (*cyfundrefn lwythol*) and as a system of land tenure (*cyfundrefn welyawg*).

* * * * * *

One of the most prominent characteristics of mediaeval Wales, at least up to the time of Owain Glyn Dŵr, was the occupation by tribal aggregations—some large and others small—of extensive territories marked by fixed and static boundaries. Many of these tribes, such as those of Marchudd ap Cynan or Cadrodd Hardd, were very old. Their origins, moreover, can often be traced back to single family settlements. The arable land of the first settlement was in time divided between the sons or grandsons of the founder, each son or grandson becoming thus the owner of a *gwely*—literally a bed or resting-place—and a founder of a *gwelygordd* (clan). In later generations, as the families associated with each clan grew in number, it became necessary to carve out of the common new arable holdings to meet increasing agricultural needs. When a clansman died, his portion of an enlarged *gwely* was subject to partible succession among his sons according to the principle which had given rise to the original *gwely*. The point to be stressed is this: expansion over a rural area by successive generations of the clan, and the continuous practice of dividing individual inheritances, did not give rise, as a rule, to new clan properties (*gwelyau*), as Seebohm maintained in his work on the " Tribal System in Wales". Every portion of land, old or new, which had been appropriated for arable use, remained a part of one of the original *gwlyau* of the tribe.

The personnel of the *gwely* was known as *gwelygordd* (clan), and in certain matters the *gwelygordd* acted as a single entity. Circuit, food and entertainment dues were assessed on the *gwely* as a whole, and consequently, until such time as tribute was commuted into money rents, collection of these dues demanded a large measure of mutual agreement within the clan. Again, every clansman enjoyed certain rights in the commons and mountain pastures of the tribal territory; and the extent of those rights could only be determined through an exact knowledge of their historical devolution in relation to similar rights enjoyed by the clansman's immediate agnatic relatives and the other members of his clan. The common rights of each clan or *gwelygordd*, moreover, had to be measured alongside those of other clans associated with it in a common tribal stock. It will be agreed that we have here sufficient mutually destructive elements to justify Gerald's observation on the attitude of brothers in Wales towards each other. But against any challenge of an external kind, the clan was united, and it was in a large measure the rules of old property law which kept this *esprit de corps* alive until the end of the fourteenth century. Still, we must beware of reading into the organisation of the *gwely* any notion of corporate ownership of the soil. Individual consciousness of possession is strong throughout the law relating to real property.

Take, for example, the principal action relating to land, which could come before a Welsh Court—the action of *ach ac edryf* (kin and descent). It is assumed in the laws that such an action will involve only individual parties; and in view of the complex nature of rights in *gwely* land, it is no surprise to find that the action is also modelled in the texts as a dispute between close kindred. The defendant could object to the plaintiff's witnesses on the ground of closer affinity to the plaintiff than to him. It was, therefore, wiser for a litigant not to bring close relatives into court to support his claim to land, although that was the procedure he was bound to follow if involved in an action of contract or suretyship or other personal actions. It was better for him to call as witnesses those who were his very distant kin, or even neighbours who were not of his own clan. The fact is that when a court was called upon to decide on rights to a piece of arable land, or to determine the more difficult problem of a clansman's share in the common pasture rights of his *gwely*, the individual clansman or *priodawr* stood isolated from his *gwelygordd* and was placed in a direct relationship with the representatives of the *state*.

Note the term *priodawr*! This was a very familar word to the lawyers of Wales in the middle ages, as well as to many who were not versed in law. A *priodawr* constituted the nearest approach in Welsh society to the feudal free-holder. The head of every constituent family of a *gwelygordd* was a *priodawr*, and he enjoyed a kind of conditional proprietorship (*priodoldeb*) in a portion of his clan's *gwely*. But the essential characteristic of this system of land tenure for the purpose of the present discussion, lay in the direct relationship already observed between every *priodawr* and the *state*. The *gwely*, no doubt, as an association of *priodorion*, facilitated the fiscal organisation of the *state*; it was without question one of the guarantees of effective order in relation to the pastoral and communal arrangements of a society organized on tribal lines; and if the *gwely* disintegrated all knowledge of the *priodorion's* rights and the conditions of their *priodoldeb* would be lost. In the last resort, however, the *state* is the ultimate guardian of the rights of the individual *priodawr* and his descendants. In consequence, the transition to the feudal idea of supreme lordship of the soil was effected without difficulty, especially as the principle of personal lordship was a traditional feature of the tribal system.

Some of the earliest legal texts can state unequivocably that there can be no land without a *brenin* (king). All proprietors were essentially men (*gwyr*) of a *brenin*. Indeed, it is clear that, in the eyes of the law, the personal tie between the king or the lord and his man, transcended the bonds of kinship. There is a very close approach here to feudal principle. Scattered references throughout the laws and the chronicles to the practice of homage (*gwrogaeth*) suggest a measure of feudal influence on the sub-structure of the tribal system. A closer analysis of the laws alone (without reference to other sources) leads to the conclusion that *gwrogaeth*, far from being merely a personal principle, was closely bound up with the principle of *priodoldeb* (proprietorship). And if there is any common principle underlying the feudal organisation of the West, it is surely the fusion of homage and proprietorship.

Notice the following customs ! A youth at the age of fourteen was presented to the lord, and having undertaken to become the lord's man, he was admitted to all the privileges of adult citizenship, or in the words of the law, he ascended to the status of a *bonheddig cynheiniawl*. On the death of the father, the lord, in a further ceremony, invests the sons with the right to divide the patrimony, and to ascend to their father's status of *priodawr*. As an acknowledgment of overlordship of the soil, the lord receives an investiture fee known as *gobr-estyn* from the heirs of the deceased proprietor. In return for this investiture, the new proprietor also recognizes the lord's right to receive annual tribute from the land, and under certain circumstances to deprive him of his proprietorship. Those who are familiar with feudal conditions in England will have observed a slight parallel between the investiture ceremony and the feudal ceremony of enfeoffment. The special circumstances which gave the lord the right to deprive a tribesman of his proprietorship, moreover, are similar to the normal feudal *incidents* of the age. If a proprietor failed to pay his annual tribute, his land reverted to the lord. The land was also forfeited if a proprietor died without an heir within the fourth degree of consanguinity, or if he was found guilty of felony or treason.

★ ★ ★ ★ ★ ★

In reviewing the conclusions reached up to this point, the feature I would stress is the function of the various tribal groupings on the eve of the English settlement of Gwynedd. The clan or *gwelygordd* as well as the more fluid system of kinship arising out of the former *galanas* organisation, were really no more than instruments for administrative and judical control by a *state* exercising direct *quasi*-feudal power over subjects without the intervention of any tribal grouping. As for the tribe or *llwyth*, it does not appear to have had any legal function or organic purpose except for the fact that there existed well-defined tribal territories within which appropriation of land by individual members of a constituent *gwelygordd* was confined. It should be realised also that although the organic bonds of the *gwely* and *gwelygordd* were weakening, the process was not yet nearly enough advanced to lessen appreciably traditional and sentimental attachments. The tribal spirit continued to exert a considerable influence on the public life of Wales for several centuries longer.

We now turn to another aspect of the subject, and one which may perhaps prove easier to grasp. Up to this point we have been delving beneath the institutional structure of mediaeval Wales,

as it were, and taking for granted the existence of the *state*. It is
proposed, therefore, to reverse the method of approach by looking
at the subject from above and in its political aspects.

* * * * * *

A Welshman in the time of Hywel Dda knew what was
meant by the terms *arglwyddiaeth* and *llywodraeth* (in modern
Welsh these terms imply lordship and government); and in the
contemporary grammar of politics there was no essential difference
between the two, as far as I can see. *Arglwyddiaeth*—that is the
personal dominion of a king—was confined to a particular *gwlad*;
and in the political constitution of Wales during the middle ages,
the *gwlad* (land) was the basic unit in the same way as *polis* or *civitas*
in the ancient world, or the *fief* in the feudal system. For centuries
the rulers of the *gwlad* had been known as *brenin* (king, *rex*). In
theory, the kings of the various *lands* of Wales (and there were many
of them) enjoyed equal status. In actual practice the power of these
kings varied considerably, and in proportion to the territorial extent
of their dominions. Boundaries were never stable. A small *gwlad*
(co-extensive with a single commote or even less) was in constant
danger of being absorbed following an attack by a stronger neighbour.
The ambition of a subject often ended in treason and treachery,
and thus caused chaos throughout the political life of the land.
Re-adjustment of boundaries was often necessary on the death of
the king, since the *gwlad* descended to all the king's sons according
to the law of *cyfran* (gavelkind) in exactly the same way as an ordinary
inheritance. This custom caused a good deal of trouble and contention,
so that major *gwledydd* were never for long at peace. Thus
it is that students of Welsh history find it difficult to keep pace with
the rapid changes in border territories between one *gwlad* and
another.

Those of you who are familar with Sir John Lloyd's classic
volumes, will find nothing new in what we have just been saying.
Such were also the features of Welsh politics in the twelfth century
which Gerald deplored. Even the law, though its aim was to overcome
anarchy, had to acknowledge the normality of civil warfare,
and to devise special means to meet crises of that kind. The law
states that if two lords, each with an army, happen to be in possession
of the same *gwlad*, and if a man should approach either of them and
request investiture of land or office or anything else, " *nid rhodd
ei rodd, ac nid estyn ei estyn* " (his gift is no gift, nor his investiture
an investiture) until this same lord should gain a victory over his
enemy.

Many *gwledydd* survived as independent units into the thirteenth
century, although by that time their number had diminished as
a result of the aggression of England on the one hand and of Gwynedd

on the other. But by then the word *brenin* (king) was no longer current, except in the older portions of the legal texts. The office and its dignity, however, remained under the new name of *arglwydd* (lord, *dominus*). There are some who maintain that the lawyers of the period did not consciously distinguish between the terms " king " and " lord ". But although I have for convenience used both terms in the same context earlier on, I believe that the lawyers of the thirteenth century knew perfectly well what was the difference between them. Indeed, in the first book of the Laws of Gwynedd the term *brenin* is used almost exclusively. That book, of course, contains the laws of the court, and as I shall try to prove later on, is made up almost entirely of archaic matter. Such is not the case with the second and third books—the laws of the country and the book of judgement. In these books *arglwydd* is the term commonly used. Occasionally " king " and " lord " appear synonymously. It is almost as if the copyist, having decided to write *arglwydd* instead of *brenin*, slips back sometimes into the form contained in the original. I do not press this point. But if I am right, what reason was there for this substitution of terms ? The answer will be found, I believe, in certain copies of *Brut y Tywysogion*.

There, the "kings" of the early entries are superseded in the first half of the twelfth century by a class of " lords ". The title " king " is reserved for the three princes who reign in Aberffraw, Mathrafal, and Dinefwr. Before the year 1154, the chronicler refers to Owen, King of Gwynedd, and to Madog ap Maredudd, King of Powys, and to Maredudd ap Rhys, King of Ystrad Tywi, Ceredigion and Dyfed. But two years after Henry II had ascended the throne of England, Owen appears in the chronicle, not as king but as Prince of Gwynedd ; while Maredudd ap Rhys's successor in the South figures as the Lord Rhys, not as Rhys the king. In 1159, Madog ap Maredudd is mentioned again, this time bearing the title of Lord of Powys. From now on, the only king referred to in the *Brut*, as far as political arrangements in Wales are concerned, is the King of England. The rulers of Powys and Deheubarth, as well as the rulers of the minor *gwledydd*, are always " lords ", wherever the chronicler has occasion to give them a specific title. Collectively they are called *tywysogion* (*principes*—a better word would be *duces*) which is an uncommon term in the chronicle before 1154, and a word which is almost entirely absent from the Laws. In fact, the term has no official significance, but is a convenient appelation for the ruling class of " lords " (the former royal class) in order to distinguish them from the leading men (*uchelwyr*) among the native freemen and the Anglo-Norman barons of the March. But at least one ruling family emerged, bearing the individual title of " prince " which had, it would appear, a constitutional significance attached to it. Owen Gwynedd was the first of that family to be Prince of

Gwynedd. The title continued to be used in the reigns of his successors, Llywelyn the Great, David ap Llywelyn and Llywelyn ap Gruffydd, until that notable year — 1267—when Llywelyn the Last had himself proclaimed *Princeps Wallie* —or in the words of the *Brut* " Prince over the whole of Wales".

The foregoing evidence suggests some form of agreement among the leading princes to drop the title of king, an understanding which co-incided with the assertion by Henry II, of the principle of Anglo-Norman lordship over Wales. A measure of political unity had already been attained when the royal title was confined to the principal courts of Wales. Now the status of the Kings of Powys and Deheubarth was reduced to the same level as that of the smaller lords. Thus in Powys and Deheubarth, a tie was broken, which had given promise of greater political unity within the framework of native institutions. The way is now left open for deeper penetration into Wales of feudal influences from across the border ; and unless those influences are withstood with more vigour than that shown by the Lord Rhys, for example, in the middle period of his career, all the *gwledydd* of Wales will be rapidly transformed into ordinary lordships on a level with the feudal lordships of England, each one directly subject to the central direction of the royal government in London. It is in this crisis that the full force and importance of Venedotian policy is revealed. Owen Gwynedd evidently felt rather uneasy about the new arrangement. He was willing to drop the royal style ; he had no objection to his fellow princes in Mathrafal and Dinefwr being reduced in rank—such a move could in the long run re-act in favour of Gwynedd ; he took an oath of homage to the English king, and as a rule his successors followed his example. But if this interpretation of the evidence is correct, Owen positively refused to be placed on the same footing as an ordinary feudal lord. The head of the royal line of Aberffraw must be accorded a special title, and to that end he adopted the style of " prince". This was a position insisted upon by all Owen's successors down to the death of Llywelyn II. However weak their political power might for a time become, they continued to style themselves Princes of Gwynedd (*principes North Wallie*). Even when Llywelyn the Great contented himself for a period with the more modest title of Lord of Snowdon, he stuck to the *princeps* in his secondary title of Prince of Aberffraw.

This was not merely a matter of *amour propre*. Behind this insistence on an official title for the ruler of Gwynedd, the influence of a genuine policy can be detected—a policy combining a sense of history and a vision of the future. At the critical moment to which reference has just been made, it was the princes of Gwynedd who halted the disaster which threatened the old political life of Wales, by borrowing ideas from the feudal world, and with the help of those who were versed in the legal traditions of Wales, using those deas in their own way to transform the existing political system into a feudal principality organised on the same unitary lines as the feudal realm in England. Their object was to build, on social foundations which were rapidly being feudalised, a political superstructure knit together constitutionally by the feudal ties of homage and fealty. Such a policy meant a great effort on the part of the northern princes to persuade and even to compel the lords of Wales to divert their allegiance from the English crown to themselves; and a still greater effort would be required to induce the King of England to acknowledge the Prince of North Wales as the only legal intermediary for the expression through oaths of homage and fealty of the feudal relationship between England and Wales. Undoubtedly, the principal objective of Venedotion policy, from Owen's day until the eclipse of Llywelyn II's hopes, was to secure for Wales, but excluding the Norman lordships in South Wales and the March, co-equal status in a federation of feudal states acknowledging the overlordship of the Anglo-Norman crown. Llywelyn the Great maintained that his status and franchise in his relations with the King of England were the same as those enjoyed by the King of Scotland. Later, Llywelyn II in a letter to the King of England wrote after this manner:—

"Each province constituted under the Empire (*imperium*) of the King of England has its own customs and laws according to the mode and use of their respective parts where they are situated, such as the Gascons in Gascony, the Scots in Scotland, the Irish in Ireland, and the English in England. I therefore seek, being a Prince, that I likewise shall have my Welsh law, and proceed according to that law. By common right, we ought to have our Welsh law and custom, as the other nations (*nationes*) in the King's Empire have—and in our own language."

I do not propose to describe how that dream was for a time realised. That subject belongs to Welsh political history, and our concern here is with the constitutional history of Wales. Details will be found in the second volume of Sir John Lloyd's *History of Wales;* and some valuable new material has become available of recent years in works published by the University Board of Celtic Studies, such as *A Calendar of Ancient Correspondence concerning Wales* and *Littere Wallie*, edited by Mr. J. G. Edwards, and *The Welsh Assize Roll*, edited by Mr. Conway-Davies. The story of the princes' bid for power is not one of unbroken success. There were many fluctuations of fortune covering the whole field of Venedotion policy before that policy was brought to a successful issue in the fleeting and uneasy triumph of Llywelyn II. But all three princes had the same aim in view, and they used like means to attain it. For example, they exerted every effort to extend the direct rule of Aberffraw over neighbouring territories; and in order to preserve that inheritance intact, they strove to abolish the custom of partible succession in respect of proprietary rights associated with the overlordship of Gwynedd. At the height of his power, in spite of the opposition of his brothers, Llywelyn II was immediate lord of Gwynedd from the Dovey to the Dee, and over many another commote to the south-east of Gwynedd, in the neighbourhood of the Wye and the Severn. Consequently, his military strength and resources were greater than those of any other Welsh lord. Then by taking every advantage (as Llywelyn the Great had done before him) of the embarrassments of the English monarchy, arising out of political strife across the border, he compelled all the lords of Wales (even the Lord of Powys himself), by fair means and foul, to transfer their homage and allegiance from the King of England to the Prince of Gwynedd. At last, in virtue of the Treaty of Montgomery, which was sealed in 1267, Llywelyn was recognized by Henry III as Prince of Wales.

On several occasions earlier in the century, a victory almost as complete as that of Llywelyn II had been won by Llywelyn the Great and his son David. One must therefore conclude that the rather primitive system of government associated in the Laws with the principal court of Gwynedd, proved insufficient during the thirteenth century to meet the administrative requirements of an enlarged principality. The remainder of the lecture will therefore be devoted to outlining those changes in the field of administration which were brought about by the political trends of the age.

★ ★ ★ ★ ★ ★

The early Laws give a prominent place to the duties and privileges of the king's officials, and to court *etiquette* in the various *gwledydd*. These rules (the Laws of the Court as they are called) appear in their original form in successive editions of the laws. Even in the thirteenth century, these rules were probably a guide to conduct in the principal court of Gwynedd, particularly on formal and ceremonial occasions. But later interpolations to the Laws of the Court, coupled with other official records of the thirteenth century, show that the essential work of the *state* was being transacted, as in England and France, by a new civil service.

Take for instance the development of the office of chancellor (*canghellor*). Apart from one late reference, there is no other mention of the chancellor in the original Laws of the Court. On the other hand the office is often referred to in the Laws of the Land as the king's chief official in the commote. At one time a local government official (for there was once a chancellor in every commote throughout Wales), the office had ceased to exist in this sense at the beginning of the thirteenth century; its functions were being everywhere executed by a new official bearing the title of *rhaglaw* or lieutenant, a much more appropriate designation, since the *rhaglaw* was the direct representative of the new *state* in the commote, and the chief administrator of the local royal estates. But that was not the end of the chancellor's office. Let us return to the reference of later date found in the Laws of the Court. In the traditional list of twenty-four court officials, another officer—*the chancellor*—appears; he claims the first place in the hall, and sits next to the king at table. A manuscript attributed to the fourteenth century adds that it is the chancellor's duty " to stand and be in the place of the king, in his presence and in his absence, in every thing; and when he is invested with office, he receives from the king a gold ring, a harp and a chess-board."

The chancellorship appears to have become the most important and dignified office at court. Indeed, by the age of the two Llywelyns it had developed into a very busy and responsible office in the court of Gwynedd. By this time, the systematic keeping of records dealing with the political and legal work of the prince's court, had become an integral part of the machinery of government in Wales. Charters, deeds, and state papers were issued in the name of the princes of Gwynedd, in almost exactly the same way as in the other feudal states of the West. Likewise, the two Llywelyns had their privy as well as their great seal. A legal commentator can in fact refer quite casually to the fees charged by the chancery " for letters patent dealing with real property and other important transactions". In fact the number and form of the curial records of thirteenth century Gwynedd prove that there existed an experienced chancery doing a considerable amount of work. The principal official responsible for this work was the chancellor (*cancellarius* in the Latin documents) So heavy did the duties of the department become that it became necessary to appoint an assistant minister—the vice-chancellor—to supervise the chancery staff — the *ysgolheigion* or *clerici*. The names of many of these clerks are known to us, and some of them travelled far afield—as far indeed as Scotland, Paris and Rome, on the diplomatic business of the Prince.

Other new officers appeared as well, and several of the older ones changed their character. In the royal courts of Hywel's day, the *gwas ystafell* (chamberlain) was the keeper of the king's treasure. But such was not the way things were ordered in the court of Gwynedd during the age of the Llywelyns. That was the period in Welsh history when fiscal problems in their modern form were beginning to creep into Wales for the first time. Llywelyn II was not a wealthy man— that is one reason why he failed to achieve permanent success. But at one time in his career he was the wealthiest prince, in every material sense, that had ever governed in Wales. The number of the royal estates was increasing; commercial organisation was being developed; the use of money for buying and selling was becoming more widespread; and the practice of discharging ancient tributes in the form of cash payments was growing more common.

Llywelyn II tried to go further and imposed upon his subjects a novel impost—a kind of income tax or capital levy—modelled on a tax which had from time to time been levied in England since the days of Henry II. The Prince's valet would no longer be competent to deal with revenue derived from so many different sources. During the century, we catch a glimpse of a new department of the prince's government dealing with fiscal business. The chief official in this department bore the same title as the head of Anglo-Norman Exchequer—the Treasurer.

Again, the office of steward (*distain*) was an honourable one in the courts of the Welsh lords. In the court of Gwynedd it developed special characteristics. The office sometimes appears as seneschal (*synysgal*) and constable (*cwnstabl*), and it gradually supplanted the old military office of *penteulu* (chief of the war-band). After the Prince, the seneschal was the principal leader of the armed forces, and to all appearances combined, in one office, the work of the chief steward and the chief constable in England. The office also tended to become hereditary as in England. Down to 1282 it was held by descendants of Ednyfed Fychan, himself steward to Llywelyn the Great and the ancestor of many of the leading county families of modern Wales.

Finally, a word about the Justice of Wales—an office corresponding in the new principality administration to that of local court judge (*ynad llys*) in the minor courts of the day. In order to arrive at a satisfactory interpretation of this office, it is necessary to pause for a moment to consider certain facts relating to the legal profession in mediaeval Wales.

It is known that an ordinary judge was free to adjudicate on many legal matters between two parties without the intervention of authority, in much the same way as a private arbitrator, provided that he had first been confirmed in the office of judge, after examination before the official judge of the local court (*ynad llys*). On the other hand, certain pleas—claims to property for example—had to be brought before the official court of the commote to be decided by an appropriate procedure in the presence of the lord or his representative, together with the court judge and some of the leading laymen of the district. At several points in the thirteenth century (as the political events of the period make evident) a large number of these local commote courts must have been linked into a single system of justice under the direction of the princes of Gwynedd. Above the commote courts there now stood the supreme court of the prince—*uchel-lys* or high court as it is called in the Laws. In this respect, the most interesting trend of the century was the emergence of a right of appeal against decisions of the commote court to the supreme court of the sovereign prince; and in some cases—especially suits relating to the authority and lands of vassal lords—this court would be one of first instance. The Prince would, of course, as overlord, preside over sessions of the High Court. The traditional procedure of the old local courts would almost inevitably leave a mark on the procedure of the central court. In the former, the official court judge took a leading part in the proceedings. It is reasonable, therefore, to regard the office of Justice of Wales as that of the *ynad-llys* writ large, and corresponding partly to the office of chief justiciar in England. Just as certain local official judges acted in relation to their local lords, so I imagine, the Justice of Wales acted in relation to the Prince—as chief counsellor in legal matters, as spokesman of the high court, as patron of the local official judges, and through the latter as principal overseer of the ordinary members of the legal profession. It is possible to imagine the existence in thirteenth century Wales of a legal hierarchy reaching its zenith in the high court.

Without much doubt, the lawyers were the chief support of the Venedotian *state*, and it was they who must have inspired much of the political programme of the princes. While a number of small semi-independent districts remained, it is true that lawyers were in such places responsible for the persistence of local customs (the variety of such customs in the extents and records of the fourteenth century is partial proof of this). But as the preambles to the legal texts make clear, the lawyers associated with the principal courts of Wales had for long been deeply conscious of a tradition of political and legal unity dating back to the days of Hywel Dda. Inspired perhaps by the legal renaissance of the twelfth century (a movement which had important repercussions on the growth of the state's power in England), and challenged by the crisis which then faced Wales, this class experienced the stirrings of national consciousness. For it is well to recollect that the sentiments which lie at the root of national consciousness, though obscured by tribal, local and provincial loyalties were never far beneath the surface in twelfth century Wales. A racial tradition of the brotherhood of all the Britons was at this time gradually giving way to the more restricted idea of the brotherhood of the Cymric or Welsh people. Echoes of the old sentiment and expressions of the new appear side by side in the *Brut*. The chronicler says of Gruffydd ap Cynan:—" King and prince and defender of the whole of Wales"; of Owen Gwynedd: " God have mercy on the British race who were foundering like a ship without a helmsman, by preserving Owen as their prince "; and again of the Lord Rhys: " The man who was the head and shield and strength of the South and of the whole of Wales, the hope and strength of all the tribes of the Britons." This is one of the last references in the chronicle to *cenedl* in one of its older meanings of *tribe*. Early in the next century *cenedl* is used for the first time in something approaching its modern meaning, and Llywelyn II can contrast the Welsh nation with other *nationes* in the letter from which a quotation was read earlier on.

It was no accident that the study of the old law of Hywel Dda flourished anew at the close of the twelfth century, for we must remind ourselves again that the earliest manuscript of the Laws has been attributed to the latter half of that century ; and from this time on, the lawyers put in a good deal of quiet work in promoting an ideal which they believed went back as far as the days of Hywel Dda. This is brought out in the earlier conclusions of this lecture, where the lawyers were seen taking every opportunity to undermine the old system of *cenedl*, so rendering it receptive to feudal influences. A close study of the Laws, it is true, reveals much conflict of law and custom between province and province. Observations such as the following occur frequently in the texts : " Some justices will have that such and such a thing is right, but we say that it is neither right nor fitting." These differences of opinion prove, moreover, the existence of a living jurisprudence, which was being thrashed out anew to meet the needs of society and of the political life of the time. But in spite of the persistence of local customs and traditions, and although some lawyers still clung to their own interpretations of the law, the teachers of law aimed at establishing uniform customs and principles. Even a cursory examination of the printed versions of the Laws, following a study of the political tendencies of the thirteenth century, serve to show that Wales was on the point of coming under the rule of a " common law " (the phraseology is again that of the Laws), when the crisis of the years 1277—1282 initiated the unequal conflict between Welsh Law and the Common Law of England.

Some of the teachers in the direct service of the court of Aberffraw by the way, ventured on ground that did not properly belong to their calling. But in the middle ages it was not uncommon to find political propaganda in works on philosophy and law. Although the royal house of Aberffraw possibly enjoyed a primacy of honour among the Welsh kings before the time of Owen Gwynedd, I feel that the stress laid in the North Wales versions of the law codes, on the paramount status of the King of Gwynedd, is deliberately overstated in order to further the ambitions of the house of Aberffraw. There is certainly no doubt that the rights claimed for the King of Aberffraw in his relations with the kings at Mathrafal and Dinefwr and with the other lords of Wales, were added to the Laws in the feudal period. As for the form of the story, introduced into some manuscripts, which describes how, on the strand at Aberdovey, Maelgwyn Gwynedd was recognized by his fellow rulers as supreme king, is it not sheer propaganda ? This is mentioned solely to emphasize the fact that the Welsh lawyers were in so many ways a really powerful force behind the struggle of the princes from the days of Owen Gwynedd until the fall of Llywelyn the Last.

The same tendencies are to be noted in the poetry of the age.*
(1) It is rare for the poets of the twelfth century to utter the word *Cymru* (Wales) and they are strangers to the word *cenedl* in its modern meaning (nation). There will be found in their work many of the elements which will in time be merged in a full consciousness of nationhood—hatred of the common foe, love of land and language, and pride in racial tradition. But the conception of a single political community under the rule of one prince is hardly there, although Gerald had actually suggested such a solution to the political problem of Wales. It is an idea which is almost always overshadowed by the poet's affection for his particular province. These sentiments, it is true, survived into the new century, and put serious practical obstacles in the way of the ideal of the house of Aberffraw. On the other hand, a remarkable feature of the age of the two Llywelyns is the new note to be found in the poetry of the court minstrels in Gwynedd.

To Dafydd Benfras, for example, Llywelyn the Great is "the great chieftain of fair Wales," and he greets him as "our common ruler." He is President of a council of feudal rulers:—

> " Llywelyn, the ruler of rulers,
> A well-mannered advocate in the council of the wise."

He is "the King of Wales," for the poets without exception cling to the traditional form of address, in spite of the constitutional changes of the time. Indeed, Dafydd Benfras claims for David ap Llywelyn (whose mother by the way was Joan, daughter of King John) rights identical with those of English kings:—

> "The grandson of the King of England, of a regal host.
> The son of the King of Wales, of equally noble lineage."

At the accession of Llywelyn ap Gruffydd, the feudal principality of Wales was to the poet an established institution; it was not merely an ideal, nor a creation of the future, but an inheritance into which Llywelyn entered according to the principles and rights of ancient Welsh Law:—

> " Sovereign son of Gruffydd
> This sovereign claims the right
> To a restored kingdom."

The Bard and the lawyer were now at one!

---

*I am deeply grateful to Mr. D. Myrddin Lloyd for valuable suggestions which are incorporated in this paragraph.

In conclusion, the functions of the "high-court" come up once more for a little further consideration. Concentrated here were all the co-ordinating elements of the feudal state. The court was not, however, merely a court of justice in the modern sense. As the supreme governing body of the feudal state, it fulfilled political and administrative functions. The letters of the princes make it evident that there was no essential difference between the court (*curia*) and the council (*concilium*). Quite as clearly the letters show that no decision of importance was taken by the princes without the advice of the chief officials of the court, members of the royal family, and the leaders of the Church in the dioceses of Bangor and St. Asaph. If the advice sought was of unusual importance, many vassal lords (the *magnates* of the Latin documents) were summoned to attend the court. On the evidence available, it is difficult to distinguish between the common-council and high-court of the Welsh princes in the thirteenth century, and the *parliamentum* of the contemporary kings of England, as the latter's constitution has been revealed to us by the research of the last half century.

In the light of what has gone before, it will be observed that Wales—*Pura Wallia* as she was called to distinguish Welsh Wales from the Anglo-Norman lordships of South Wales and the March— had developed in every direction all the characteristics of a feudal state in miniature when the hopes of the princes were shattered by the Treaty of Conway in 1277, and by the tragedy near Builth in 1282.

T. JONES-PIERCE.

FROM THE FALL OF LLYWELYN TO THE TUDOR PERIOD.

IT gives me great pleasure to take part in an Ysgol Haf given over entirely to a survey of the past of Wales. Such a survey, in my opinion, is long overdue, for we, the Welsh people, have been too long estranged from our historic past. In this we differ calamitously from our sister nation beyond the sea; for whenever a comparison is made between the two Celtic nations of Wales and Ireland, a difference that is invariably pointed out is that Ireland is a country that has kept her history and forgotten her language, while Wales has kept her language but forgotten her history. And there was a time perhaps when the comparison was true in all its aspects, but today, Wales is a country which is fast thrusting its language into the same limbo to which she has consigned her history. This should not surprise us, for the slave has no rights of possession and readily allows himself to be despoiled of any treasures that remain to him from the time when he had not yet been degraded.

As Nationalists, we have many duties to our nation, and not the least is the duty of restoring a sense of her historic past. But in this act of restoration we must be aware of one thing, namely, that we are a subject nation and that for centuries our past has been interpreted for us by our rulers, or by those of our own people who have been educated in the schools of our conquerors. That is, the historic past of this nation of ours has been presented to us, and is being presented, as it is seen through English eyes. This is a fact which every subject nation must face: that the history of a conquered nation is always expressed in terms of the conqueror. Notice how Fichte expresses the situation: " A country that has lost its independence has lost therewith the power of intervening in the stream of time and of independently determining its course. So long as it remains in this condition, its destiny, its very chronology are measured off by the foreign Power that rules its fate, and henceforth it has not even a history of its own, but reckons its years according to the incidents and epochs of foreign peoples and kingdoms." Further, its conquest is invariably represented as a civilising process, with the conqueror playing the role of the apostle of a superior civilisation to a primitive and barbaric people. We have to remember that we have all been subjected to an English system of education, and as a result even Welsh historians instinctively, and perhaps unconsciously, look at Wales through English eyes, and repeatedly reveal a strong English bias in their interpretation of the facts of Welsh history,—compare, for example, the general attitude of historians to Llywelyn the Last, who " grasped the shadow and lost the substance," and their general refusal to take up a correspondingly critical attitude towards Edward I's highly provocative behaviour towards Llywelyn. Or again, has any Welsh historian failed to join in the applause accorded by English historians to Edward I's "statesmanlike" ambition to unite the whole island under English rule? As Nationalists, we know that there *is* another point of view with regard to this "statesmanlike" attitude. In other words, the historical impartiality about which we have heard so much in Wales is not so universally in operation as we have fondly supposed. And, indeed, it may be doubted whether an utterly scientific impartiality in dealing with history is either possible or desirable; it is to be doubted, also, whether the historian's preoccupation with impartiality is as unassailable as we Welsh have been led to believe. Sir Charles Oman, the English historian, actually declared that the historian's prejudices are valuable, while certain Continental scholars, such as F. A. Hayek, believe that the historian's attempts at impartiality, at presenting the facts without taking sides, has been an undiluted tragedy. For the historian *must* take sides, he must praise or blame, and that openly, not subtly as the English historian does. He must establish a standard of values, whereby the facts of history may be assessed, for it is the historian who moulds the public conscience, whether he will or not, and since he has, hitherto, withheld judgment, the people, deprived of a sound standard, have taken the worst possible standard for judging the facts of history, namely, their success. There is only one true standard by which the people may judge and which the historian may use without fear that his bias will pervert his presentation of the facts, and that is the moral standpoint.

The standpoint of success has been generously used in adjudging the history of Wales, and that is why the pro-English bias is so obvious in the usual presentation of Welsh history, and as Nationalists we must re-assess and re-interpret our history and insist upon applying the moral touchstone to the facts of our past. After all, is it so desperate a crime for a Welshman to look at the history of his own nation through Welsh eyes, or to handle it with love or pride or sorrow instead of with an impartiality so rigidly cold as to become positively hostile? This is how, we are told, the great Danish philosopher Grundtvig looked at Denmark: "He did not wish any subject, Denmark least of all, in any phase of her life to be dissected and analysed critically and statistically. It was a personal human Denmark that he wished to have shown to the people, her limitations and weaknesses not ignored, but touched with a loving insight, her spirit set forth in the light of poetry and high hopes which would thrill all youth to its best service in her behalf." "Touched with a loving insight." Shall we err so badly if we too insist upon treating Wales and her historic past in this way?

In the period about which I wish to speak, Wales was a subject nation and had been a subject nation for almost a century. The official documents from which the history of our nation has been compiled were drawn up by our rulers, and as such they express the point of view of the conqueror. We see Wales through Anglo-Norman and English eyes. The patriotic readiness of the nation to rise to regain its freedom or to resist acts of oppression and injustice are stigmatised as "lightness of head"; the patriot is described as a turbulent rebel and breaker of the law, the collaborator is applauded as a good and loyal subject. Dafydd Gam is knighted and applauded, Owain Glyn Dŵr is treated with odium as a greedy rebel baron, a fanatic dreamer of fantastic dreams.

In order to gain a sense of balance, we must try to discover what the subject people felt. In Wales, luckily, for us, there was a numerous and highly educated community of very active people in this period, the bards, who regarded poetry as a social function, and as such, their work is a valuable asset to us in trying to see Wales, not as she appeared to her rulers, but as she appeared to her children. Bardic literature is very abundant and was the only place where Wales could express herself. I intend to talk to you today not about Wales as she appeared to her rulers—you can get that view in any history book—but as she appeared to her own children in those difficult centuries when her pride had not yet been broken, and when she still refused to submit to the indignity of being the hewer of wood and the drawer of water in the house of her conqueror.

One of the dark hours in the history of Wales (and we have known many such hours) came on that early December day, in 1282, when Llywelyn ap Gruffudd, Prince of Gwynedd, Llywelyn the Last, was slain near Builth. His tragic death was greeted by the bards with bitter lamentation, the most moving and poignant in its grief and despair being the fine elegy of Gruffudd ab yr Ynad Coch, in which the personal sorrow of the poet and the agony of the nation in its hour of despair are beautifully portrayed. Llywelyn's death had the effect of throwing the nation into a torpor (relieved only by the minor risings of Madog ap Llywelyn and Gruffydd Llwyd in North Wales, and of Llywelyn Bren in the South) out of which it was only beginning to come in the time of Dafydd ap Gwilym some fifty years later, to remember its martial ability, and to remember that something better awaited it than an abject prostration under the heel of a conqueror.

Dafydd ap Gwilym himself was not politically minded, and he seems sublimely unaware of Welsh nationhood and of patriotism as bards younger than he were to know and express them. This does not mean that the Welsh had not advanced far along the road to nationhood, for his case can be paralleled by hundreds of similar cases in Wales today. Dafydd belonged to a family which stood well with the English or Anglo-Normans in the country, for an uncle of his, Llywelyn ap Gwilym, was deputy constable at Newcastle Emlyn in 1343, and Dafydd had nothing but friendly feelings for the rulers. In Dafydd's work, therefore, the nearest approach to a sense of nationality is a dim consciousness that the English in Wales were something to be laughed at; he mocks at them "the monstrous low-born English men," with the same aristocratic contempt that he turns upon the unfree of his own race. That is all we get from Dafydd: an aristocratic contempt for a race of boors, but before the end of the century in which he lived, there emerged, for the first time since the fall of Llywelyn, a political nationalism which instantly gripped the people and grew in strength and intensity throughout the fifteenth century, reaching its peak in the victory of Bosworth, and effectually driving away the last vestiges of their stupor. The roots of the political nationalism which became so prominent during the fifteenth century, lay in the consciousness of nationhood which can be traced at least as far back as the beginning of the thirteenth century, and throughout the later Middle Ages, Wales grew steadily in the knowledge of herself as a nation, a knowledge which is expressed in Welsh literature of these periods.

During the century following Llywelyn's death, the Welsh began to flow in increasing numbers into the armies of other lands. At first, they were compelled by Edward I to join his armies to fight in Scotland and on the Continent, and they soon won a reputation for themselves as impetuous and fiery soldiers, whose national weapon, the longbow, was something to be feared. When Edward III began the Hundred Years' War for the throne of France, it was natural for him also to conscript Welsh troops for the war, and their longbows at Crecy won a famous victory for the king of England. The Welsh bards of the day were quite ready to praise the exploits of those Welshmen who won fame and rewards for themselves in fighting for the English. Indeed, Iolo Goch, a contemporary of Dafydd ap Gwilym, was hardly less careless of patriotism than Dafydd himself; so careless that he could find it in his heart to write a poem in praise of the English king himself, Edward III, whose only lively interest in Wales was in the conscripting of her fighting men, and he could even comment approvingly that Edward possessed the qualities of his grandfather, Edward I. When we remember that Edward I was the man who had completed the conquest of Wales and by his establishment of privileged English boroughs in the land had effectually shackled the whole economic and commercial life of the country until the Act of Union, 1536, we can appreciate the depth of Iolo's unpatriotic fervour. Yet even Iolo was not always to be found at this level, and in his day a change took place, a change which roused Wales from her apathy and indifference to her fate, a change for which bards of a very different temper from Dafydd ap Gwilym and Iolo Goch were largely responsible, and henceforth, we find the bardic classes playing a vital part in the political life of the nation.

A virile consciousness of nationhood and of a long and illustrious historic past in a nation oppressed by another is bound to find expression, sooner or later, in a political nationalism of a more or less militant nature, and Wales in our period was no exception to the rule. The bards from the later fourteenth century onwards were as a class animated by two great passions : an ardent devotion to their own country and a deep hostility towards England, and they became the indefatigable propagandists of the movement which began in the later fourteenth century. In the latter half of this century, the bards deliberately set about the task of rousing Wales to take up arms again on behalf of her freedom and for this purpose they made use of an old prophecy that a hero named Owain would some day come from over the sea to conquer the Saxons, to drive them back whence they had come, and to restore the ancient glories of the Brythons. This prophecy was now used on behalf of definitely historical figures, most of whom at the zenith of their power, were acclaimed by the bards, each in his turn, as the undoubted Son of Prophecy, y Mab Darogan, the long-expected Owain.

The beginning of bardic propaganda coincided with the appearance of a Welsh hero whose possibilities as the Owain of Prophecy instantly arrested the attention of the bards, though he appeared from a most unexpected quarter. After the peace of 1360, which brought a temporary lull in the war between France and England, Free Companies began to be formed on the Continent, composed of hardy veterans of war, who obeyed none but their chosen leader and sold their services to the highest bidder. Many of these companies were composed entirely of Welshmen to whom this free life of fighting and plunder was preferable to life in Wales with all its disabilities and restrictions, where they were liable to serve in the English army at a low rate of pay. It is as a leader of a company of Welshmen fighting on the French side, that we find the most outstanding Welshman of the period, Owain ap Thomas ap Rhodri, whom the Welsh called Owain Lawgoch. Owain's grandfather, Rhodri, was a brother of Llywelyn the Last, and had been taken to England as a hostage when a child, and had lived and died there. In 1277, Edward I had given him an English estate, and he and his son Thomas were to all intents and purposes English gentlemen. Thomas had a small estate in Montgomeryshire, however, and did once make an attempt to claim some of the patrimony of his family in North Wales. As the sole remaining male descendant of the Royal House of Gwynedd. Owain seems to have been brought up in France and only once appeared in Wales,—in 1363, when he returned after his father's death to claim his father's estates. But that once was enough. The bards had found a living member of the family of Llywelyn the Last, one who was, moreover, a dashing soldier, with as little love for the English as the bards themselves. It is unlikely that the bards missed the opportunity of making the acquaintance of this scion of the family of Llywelyn (of whose existence few seem to have known during his father's life), and their contact undoubtedly influenced both Owain and the bards deeply. Owain left behind him a community of skilful propagandists working on his behalf, while the bards ennobled the prince's ambitions with a vision of himself as the longed-for deliverer of a subject nation.

In 1369, on the renewal of the war, Owain threw in his lot with France. His appearance altered the whole aspect of the war for Wales, and for her, the war in France now assumed the proportions of a national movement to regain her freedom under the guidance of a prince of the ancient line of Gwynedd. From now on, Welsh soldiers in France definitely took the French side; Owain's appeal overcame all other considerations with them, and even Ieuan Wyn, who had won fame on the English side, threw in his lot with his fellow-countrymen. In Wales, the work of preparing the Welsh people was already under way, and in 1370 we find a certain Gruffydd Says compelled to forfeit all his land in Anglesey for being a supporter of Owain Lawgoch. By 1372, we find that Owain has obtained command of a French naval force, not for the invasion of England, but for the recovery of Wales, which, as he states in a proclamation that year, he claimed "by right of succession, by kindred, by heritage and by right of descent from my ancestors, the kings of that country." He describes how he had gone begging assistance from court to court and had been given the means of equipping a fleet by the French king for the purposes of recovering his kingdom and of avenging himself upon the king of England for the wrongs done to him and his ancestors.

Six weeks after this proclamation, the way was opened for Owain's expedition by the destruction of the English fleet off La Rochelle. The popular attitude in Wales towards Owain is reflected in a poem, by Gruffydd ap Maredudd,[1] possibly written in 1372 when Owain was about to invade Wales. The poet is full of eager anticipation of his coming and is confident that Owain, " King of Wales," will gain the support of all Wales and inflict a crushing defeat upon the English. Another poet proclaims that the time for the fulfilment of the prophecies has come and for Wales to regain her freedom. " This is the year," he asserts gleefully, " when the White Dragon shall take flight with the Red Dragon in pursuit."[2] These poems show that the long years of hopeless defeat and of sullen submission were at an end, and that Wales was waking to the realisation that she might yet throw off the yoke of England. A leader had presented himself, one who possessed all the qualities likely to appeal to the imagination of bard and people alike : he was of the Royal House of Gwynedd, determined to recover the kingdom of Wales wrested from his ancestors, and was, moreover, famous for his military powers, and feared by the English.

1. R.B.P. col. 1313—1314.
2. Iolo Goch ac Eraill.—xxxiii.

There seemed every likelihood, when Owain set out from Harfleur, that he would succeed in his enterprise, but he got no further than Guernsey, which he overran with comparative ease. At this point, however, the French king saw an opportunity of conquering La Rochelle and Poitou and sent a message to Owain requiring his return. Owain wavered, but his old instincts and his whole previous life proved too much for him, and the newly discovered national leader, sailing to right old wrongs and to reclaim his kingdom, was lost in the soldier of fortune. Owain obeyed the king of France, and returned to France before he could test the temper of his people. For some years, Wales waited, feeding on rumours of invasion, and then, in 1378, came the news that an agent of the English government, John Lamb, had assassinated him while he was besieging Mortaigne-sur-Garonne.[3]

His death was a sore disappointment to Welsh hopes, so much so that even a century later, poems were written, recalling the eager preparations, the selling of cattle and farm implements to buy horses and armour, the long watching of the sea for Owain's coming, the agony of despair when his death became known. But the whole affair had one important result, it had shaken Wales out of her long stupor and fired her imagination. Even today, Owain is believed to be like Arthur, sleeping in a cave until Wales shall call upon him. His connection with France was to be of some benefit also to his successor and greater namesake, Owain Glyn Dŵr. The Welsh of the fourteenth and fifteenth centuries were incurable optimists. In spite of defeat after defeat and the repeated destruction of their most cherished hopes, they never despaired altogether, or lost all faith in the prophecies that inspired them. After Owain's death, Llywelyn ap Cynfrig Ddu of Anglesey declared that Owain Lawgoch was not the Son of Prophecy, for the signs of the latter's coming had not yet been fulfilled. Therefore, though Owain Lawgoch had been slain, God would raise another Owain to deliver Wales.

The Welsh, on Owain's death, were once more leaderless, but no longer apathetic; he had bequeathed to them at least a hope for the future, and taught them that despairing submission to the conqueror was not the only course open to them. Besides, " fifty years of fighting other people's battles in Scotland and on the Continent had, at any rate, given him (the Welshman) a revived consciousness of his ability to fight."[4] Wales had been prepared, physically and mentally, for a national movement greater than any before. There remained but to find the leader, who would take up the cause where Owain Lawgoch had left it. She had not long to wait before finding another Owain as the rallying point for the national movement. This was Owain ap Gruffydd Fychan, better known as Owain Glyn Dŵr, best loved of all the heroes of Wales.

---

3. Tr. Cym. 1899—1900.
4. Tr. Cym. 1925—26. Article by D. L. Evans.

Owain was the heir of the princes of Powys Fadog, and was linked with the royal houses of the South and the North. He was indeed of the royal blood of all Wales, though his position in his own day was merely that of a minor marcher lord holding, direct from the English Crown, lands which his ancestors had ruled as Princes. Owain Glyn Dŵr is the most enigmatic of all the great leaders of Welsh history, and praise and blame alike have been heaped upon him. He has been described as the unsuccessful rebel, the ill-starred victim of ambition, whose career was well fitted to point the moral of the vanity of human aspirations, as the greedy baron who involved a whole country in ruin for the sake of his personal ambition. The nation which suffered the ruin, however, shared none of these doubts and scruples; they flocked to his standard and in his adversity no one was found who would betray him to his enemies. All Wales welcomed his rising as a continuation of the national struggle begun by Owain Lawgoch.

It was once thought that a great deal of poetry addressed to Owain by the bards of his day has survived. This is not so; extant literature is disappointingly meagre in reference to Owain. What little has survived, however, gives us an attractive picture of our great hero. We see him in his dashing youth in glittering armour, going off to Scotland,—in the army of Richard II. (of all the unexpected places to find him); we catch a glimpse of him in gorgeous apparel engaged in the jousting so popular in his day, and we see him in the pleasant happiness of his home at Sycharth, living the peaceful, hospitable life of the Welsh country gentleman in the midst of his family, with no shadow to mar his happiness. He was the perfect Welsh gentleman: bold and stern when necessary, kindly to the poor and helpless, unfailing in his gracious courtesy and so gentle that he would not pretend to take a toy from a child in fun lest he cause it pain. The conversation at Sycharth in those happy years was not always peaceful and did not always concern the small world of a little Welsh lordling, and the odes to which Owain listened were not all of them compliments to his hospitality, his gentlemanly accomplishments, and the ancient lineage from which he had sprung. Sometimes they dealt with the fate of an ancient and aristocratic nation. Gruffydd Llwyd, for example, the great poet of the day, addressed a poem to Owain about 1386, describing the wretched and oppressed state of Wales, her ancient glories, her need of a leader to raise her fallen fortunes and pointing out that she possessed none but Owain to lead her now. A plain hint that would not be lost on a Welsh noble of royal blood. Owain cannot but have known before 1400 that he had but to rise and the nation would rise with him. Obviously, too, the bards had decided that Owain Glyn Dŵr was to be the next leader in the fight for freedom, and were already preparing him for the course he took when the personal quarrel with Lord Grey, his neighbour, gave him a pretext for action which would test the temper of the nation.

In September, 1400, Owain raised his standard. The actual occasion of the war seems to have been the high-handed conduct of his neighbour, Lord Grey of Ruthin, in seizing a portion of Owain's inheritance, an offence for which Owain failed to get any redress in the English law courts. The war, however, speedily assumed national proportions, becoming a rising such as Wales had not seen since the days of Llywelyn. Owain himself issued a proclamation in which he described the object of the revolt: " to deliver the offspring of Wales out of the captivity of our English foes, who have for a long time past oppressed us and our ancestors." The Welsh flocked to his support and at first he swept all before him, nearly succeeding in achieving his object, and in restoring the freedom of Wales. He made his headquarters at Harlech when at the height of his power, and in 1404 summoned a council of representatives from all Wales to Machynlleth. This Council conferred on Owain the title Prince of Wales. Owain was astute enough to realise that he could not fight without allies, so he made an alliance with the Percy family of Northumberland, enemies of Henry IV, and he caused the Council to send ambassadors to France to arrange a treaty. After 1405, his strength began to decline, his sons were slain and he himself beseiged in Harlech Castle. By 1412, it was no longer possible to carry on the struggle. When Henry V came to the throne of England, he was soldier enough to appreciate an indomitable foe, and he offered Owain and his most outstanding captains a free pardon. But Owain scorned to accept a pardon from the king of England for fighting the cause of his own nation. He disappeared, no one knows whither, and no one knows to this day where his body lies.

Owain's Rising had failed, the only visible results being a country devastated by war, and Henry IV's stringent re-enactment of Edward I's special ordinances against the Welsh. Yet O wain had shown himself to be a great statesman, whose vision of what Wales should be has been the goal towards which Wales has ever since progressed. There have been times, in the long centuries since, when his vision has become dimmed, but it has not been quite forgotten, even in our most degraded moments. His naional ideals appear in a letter written to Charles VI of France. They were : (1) that Wales was to be independent of England, and under Owain, assisted by a Council of representatives from all Wales ; (2) the Church in Wales to be independent of Canterbury, and St. David's to be the seat of its archbishopric ; (3) two universities to be established, one in South Wales and one in the North. These noble ideals left Owain high above the ranks of the sordid self-seeking rebels, and Wales has had to wait many centuries before seeing even a partial fulfilment of them.

To the English, some of whom had been involved in the impenetrable mists of the Berwyns or had noticed how inclement the weather was when Henry IV led them into Wales against the great

Welshman, Owain became a great magician, who could command the elements to do his will! To the Welsh he became the symbol of the national spirit, indomitable against tremendous odds, an inspiration for all time. The Tudor chronicler, Elis Gruffydd relates a tradition that Owain had stayed at Valle Crucis shortly before his disappearance, and one morning, chancing to go out walking early and meeting the abbot, he said, "Ah, Sir Abbot, you have risen too early." "No," said the Abbot, "it is you who has risen too early by a hundred years," meaning that Owain Glyn Dŵr was not the deliverer of prophecy, and as a result (according to Elis), Owain shortly afterwards disappeared. His dauntless courage and uncertain end were a matter of pride and hope to his countrymen for many years, and it was long ere they gave up hoping that, in the words of the poet, " Owain shall rise again."

The years following the Rising were difficult years for the Welsh ; the penal laws were enforced more strictly than ever, and the land groaned under the tyranny of the English officials. The suffering of the nation at this time is reflected in a poem to Rhys Gethin, one of Owain's captains :

> Byd caeth ar waedoliaeth da
> A droes, aml oedd drais yma;
> Lle bu'r Brython, Saeson sydd
> A'r boen ar Gymru beunydd. (Iolo Goch ac Eraill xli.)

> The world has become a place of bondage to those of good blood, frequent are the acts of oppression. Where once the Brython was, the English now are, and pain is the daily lot of Wales.

We hear much about the tyrannous English officials in Wales in the fifteenth century from the bards, who repeatedly express the yearning of the Welsh people for freedom from their harshness, and implore all the nobles who rise into prominence to rescue the nation from their clutches. Over and over again they tell the gentry such things as " you have the key to lock up the English so that they cannot obtain office " :

> Chwi a ellwch â'ch allwydd
> Roi clo ar Sais rhag cael swydd. (Gwaith Ieuan Deulwyn xxix.)

Even the bow and arrows are to the bards " Gelynion Saeson a'u swydd," the enemies of the English and their office. Lewis Glyn Cothi hopes that one of his patrons will begin a new era when the Saxons shall no longer be holding sessions or official positions, and will be deprived of all their splendour, while Guto'r Glyn complains to Edward IV that the Welsh are born in servitude, the prey of thieves, and implores him to come to their rescue and curb the evil ones:

> Gwae ni o'n geni yn gaeth
> Gan ladron, gwna lywodraeth;
> Dyred, dy hun, Edwart hir
> I ffrwyno cyrff rhai anwir. (Gwaith Guto'r Glyn lvi.)

There is a tendency to suggest that the severity of the Penal Laws has been over-rated and that on the cessation of hostilities the worst of them were over though they remained on the statute book till the time of James I. This tendency is not supported by the facts, however; they were certainly enforced quite stringently in the fifteenth century and were twice renewed during the century. If there was any relaxation, it must have come during the Wars of the Roses, when civil war had paralysed the government and rendered it incapable of enforcing measures against the Welsh people. In general, the government showed itself readier to accede to the demands of the North Wales boroughs for a tightening of the ordinances than to notice Welsh requests to be rid of their disadvantages. It was not easy for Welshmen to obtain denizenship, that is, equal privilege with Englishmen in Wales, and that in itself points to a reluctance to remove the disabilities from the shoulders of the Welsh people, except in the case of an unusually powerful Welshman, such as Gruffydd ap Nicholas. A Welshman seeking denizenship had to submit to a betrayal of his nationality and prove, like William Fychan of Penrhyn, that he was part English in blood. Indeed, the means of obtaining denizenship were sufficiently unworthy to win the strongest disapproval of the bards and might be accompanied by such restrictions as that they must not marry Welshwomen. Guto'r Glyn is moved to sorrow at sight of Welshmen who wished to gain citizenship:

> Ac eraill gynt a gerais
> A bryn swydd a breiniau Sais. (Ibid lxviii.)

Englishman.
Other whom once I loved, buy the office and the privilege of an

These restrictions served no good purpose, but simply intensified the cleavage between Wales and England; a cleavage faithfully reflected in Welsh literature, which breathes a spirit of deep hatred towards the English unparalleled in any other period. The natural consequences of a policy of repression against a conquered people is another rebellion on the part of the repressed, but that was a course which the Welsh found impossible for years after the Glyn Dŵr Rising owing to the exhausted state of the country. Under such circumstances, it was natural for the weaker and less independent spirits to submit, and we find many Welshmen escaping from the disabilities of life in Wales by joining the English army and going to fight once more in France. The more daring and independent among the Welsh took to the woods and the fastnesses of the hills to await the time when Owain should once more appear. For many of these people were convinced that Owain was not dead but simply lurking in hiding awaiting a favourable opportunity of continuing his rising. These followers of Owain, " gwerin Owain " as they were called, formed a nucleus around which gathered the numerous bands of outlaws who lived in the woods with their hand mainly directed against the English as their legitimate prey.

The Welsh strongly resented the disabilities under which they laboured and rioting was common. The most serious riot occurred in 1442, and the ring-leaders were Ifan ap Robin in Caernarvonshire, Sir Gruffydd Fychan in the Valley of the Dee, and Owain ap Gruffydd ap Nicholas in the South. These were all outlawed for their part in the affair, together with some " militant monk," possibly one of the bards, who had been stirring up the people. The riot was doomed to failure, and nothing came of it except the order of Parliament in 1444 for the stricter observance of all statutes ever enacted against the Welsh. There seems to have been no attempt to look into the causes of the revolt, and no curb put upon the English officials. Indeed, the years between the disappearance of Owain Glyn Dŵr and the outbreak of the Wars of the Roses were a time of difficulty, of lawlessness and feuds (originating in hostility between those who had supported Owain and those who had opposed him) that is unparalleled in all Wales's previous history. But in spite of everything, the people clung tenaciously to the belief that better times lay ahead and their faith in the coming of the Son of Prophecy was unshaken. The bards, too, worked energetically to sustain the hopes of the nation. In the midst of the most difficult years of this part of the fifteenth century, appeared the most gallantly hopeful of all the poems written to assert an undaunted faith in the future of the Welsh nation. This poem, attributed, probably incorrectly, to Siôn Cent, laments the sad state of Wales, fated to suffer constant wrong, once held in great respect now at a low ebb, and possessing neither houses nor lands. " It is strange that my thoughts do not kill me," says the poet, " but I am in hope for that which is to come " ; " Gobeithiaw a ddaw ydd wyf." Throughout the rest of this long poem in which the story of the nation and its illustrious past is traced, this is the constantly recurring refrain :

" Gobeithiaw a ddaw ydd wyf." (I.G.E. xciv.)

The faith in the coming of the deliverer grew ever stronger as the century advanced. At first, the return of Glyn Dŵr was expected, but as the fifteenth century wore on and hope faded that Glyn Dŵr would ever return, the bards skilfully diverted the expectation of the people to the Owain of the book of prophecies.

Throughout the century, they watched eagerly for one who might become the national leader, and when the Wars of the Roses broke out in England, involving many Welsh gentry also, they redoubled their efforts to make use of this most sordid war as a bid for freedom. They clearly regarded this war as a continuation of the Glyn Dŵr Rising, repeatedly urging Welsh leaders to continue the work of Glyn Dŵr and begging them not to sheathe the sword of Owain of the Glen : " Na weinia gledd Owain Glyn." They directed Welsh attention quite impartially to the Lancastrian Tudors and the Yorkist Herberts of Gwent and even to Edward IV, who had some Welsh blood in him, as each in turn became prominent, extolling them as national leaders and imploring them to restore Welsh freedom.

After the death of Owain Glyn Dŵr, the hopes of the nation gradually became centred upon the Tudor family of Penmynydd in Anglesey, and the bards began to believe that the deliverer would spring from this stock. Owain Tudor, who married Queen Catherine, widow of Henry V, about 1430, was the first to engage their attention, while his sons, Edmund and Jasper, were also early acclaimed prospective leaders of the nation in its bid for freedom. Edmund's early death filled the bards of all Wales, the South no less than the North, with gloom, but their hopes revived at the posthumous birth of his son, Henry. All was not lost, there would still be a leader when Henry grew up. Jasper, too, was the centre of bardic hopes after his brother's death until his own defeat at Mortimer's Cross in 1461.

Meanwhile, another Welshman was rising into prominence, William Herbert of Raglan, who became Earl of Pembroke. After Mortimer's Cross, the Yorkists were strong, and correspondingly interesting to the Welsh bards, and William Herbert became the most popular hero in Wales, and his reputation as a soldier won him the esteem of the bards, who pinned their hopes upon him instead of the Tudors, and earnestly exhorted him to further the cause of Wales. Indeed, in reading Welsh literature in the period, we lose sight of the partisan nature of the Wars of the Roses. Lewis Glyn Cothi of South Wales, for example, who had urged on the Tudors before Herbert's rise and was to do so again after his death, was equally wholehearted in extolling William Herbert and in winning Welsh support for him. Dafydd Llwyd of North Wales, an eager partisan of the Tudors, was yet as sincere as all the other bards in mourning the battle in which William Herbert was slain. Wales was the real affection of these bards and they could not bear to see even the leader they were supporting at the moment, punishing his countrymen who would not join him. Dafydd Llwyd pleads with Edward IV, "Be merciful, oh valiant Welshman, to the fair Welsh," and points out that Paul had once opposed Jesus and Mary Magdalene been unchaste. Similarly, Guto'r Glyn in 1468, addresses a fine poem to William Herbert, who had recently been devastating in

Gwynedd, in which he gives striking expression to the sense of the national unity of Wales, and of the distinction between Wales and England. He shows the same transcendent love of Wales as Dafydd Llwyd and the same pain when any of her sons are made to suffer, especially by the leader whom he expects to deliver Wales. It is obvious that he disapproves of William Herbert's assumption of the rôle of Yorkist leader and of his punishment of those Welsh who supported the Lancastrian faction; rather, Herbert's duty was to unite all Wales in the struggle for Welsh freedom. He too reminds Herbert of the merciful treatment meted out to Paul of old and appeals to Herbert also to show mercy even though Gwynedd has been disobedient. Like other bards of his day, Guto'r Glyn clearly regarded York and Lancaster as of no account in the relations of Welshmen with each other; the great unifying factor was Wales and her freedom. His poem gives perhaps the finest utterance in the whole period to an abiding sense of nationhood. He ends with his famous appeal to William Herbert, to unite all Wales under his rule, and to free it from the domination of the English and their privileges:

> Cymer wŷr Cymru'r awron,
> Cwnstabl o Farnstabl i Fôn;
> Dwg Forgannwg a Gwynedd
> Gwna'n un o Gonwy i Nedd;
> O digia Lloegr a'i dugiaid
> Cymru a dry yn dy raid. (Guto'r Glyn lvi.)

William Herbert was not long to remain in his glory; in July 1469, he and his brother Richard, took part in the battle of Banbury and lost the day. Large numbers of Welshmen were slain and captured and about 168 Welshmen of note are said to have fallen. The Herbert brothers were among the prisoners, and were both executed without any opportunity of ransom. The death of the Earl and of so many of the flower of Welsh nobility was greeted as a national calamity and no one in Wales thought of it as a party reverse. All the famous bards of the day wrote a lament to those who fell in the battle. Dafydd Llwyd, in adding his voice to the general lament, suggests that there is now a hope for the return of Henry Tudor to take vengeance upon the fickle hosts of Edward and Warwick. It is an interesting indication of the attitude of the Welsh bards that Dafydd can regard the return of the Lancastrian Henry Tudor as vengeance for the death of the Yorkist Herberts. Llywelyn ap Hywel of Llantrisant in Glamorgan shared the same view and he too ended his fine elegy to the nobles who fell at Banbury upon the same note of hope struck by Dafydd Llwyd. The awakening will come from over the sea whence Jasper Tudor will come. Llywelyn mourns not the death of any one member of the nobility of Wales, but all who fell in that dark week. He voices the sorrow and gloom that prevailed in Wales ; once more the old prophecies have been frustrated in the hour of victory and nothing remains but to bid farewell to the pleasures of life, to green garments and silk and gold, to songs and dirges, for there are no earls and knights to ask them of us. There must be a farewell also to feasting. It is useless to think of building castles any more, or to have estates, for no man will require them, but merely want to build a cottage of bracken.

After Banbury, Wales found herself once more brought to the verge of ruin ; William Herbert had gone the way of Owain Lawgoch, of Owain Glyn Dŵr and Owain Tudur. The memory of Banbury lingered long, but the bards began again to seek a leader, one who would at last bring her constantly frustrated hopes to fruition. For a time the bards even toyed with the idea of seeking the assistance of Edward IV, for the fulfilment of Welsh hopes, and more than one poem was addressed to him, urging him to alleviate the sufferings of Wales, to restore her ancient laws and to be the deliverer so much longed for. After Banbury, however, the bulk of the Welsh nation turned more and more towards Jasper and Henry Tudor for the fulfilment of the prophecies. After the battle of Tewkesbury, 1471, Jasper and Henry were in exile on the Continent, and during the long years of their absence, the bards industriously prepared Wales to support Henry, composing innumerable prophetic poems in which they claimed Henry as the expected Owain. These poems revived the long deferred hopes of the nation, stirred the martial spirit of the people and fanned their longing for the freedom of Wales, and for vengeance upon the English for all the suffering they had caused. The political nationalism expressed in these poems was acceptable to all Wales, the South as well as the North. As the time for Henry's coming drew near, the bards grew bolder and spoke openly and fearlessly. The whole land was aflame with expectation and there was much anxious watching of the coast for the appearance of his fleets. Dafydd Llwyd expects Jasper to take part in the great deliverance :

Siaspar in a ddarparwyd
Ynte yn rhydd a'n tyn o'r rhwyd, (Tr. Cym. 1917—18, p.45.)

while an unknown poet addressed an appeal to Henry to come forth from his hiding place to conquer the Mole (Richard III) and to free Wales from her previous bonds :

" Dwg ni o'n rhwym dygn yn rhydd." Iolo Goch (Ashton)xiv.

Henry Tudor was well aware of the preparations made for his coming in Wales and on August 7th, 1485, he landed at Milford Haven. He unfurled the Red Dragon as his standard and announced rather ambiguously that he had come " to free this our Principality of Wales of such miserable servitude as they have long piteously stood in." All this could have but one meaning for Wales,—that Henry was leading a national war of liberation,—and Henry himself must have known it. As he traversed Wales on his way to Shrewsbury, men flocked to his side and on August 22nd, he won the battle of Bosworth, with a predominantly Welsh army, and slew Richard III of England. His victory was hailed with delirious joy in Wales as the end of the afflictions of the Cymry and the beginning of the freedom of Wales. Gruffydd ab Ieuan ap Llywelyn Fychan wrote confidently of the victorious Henry that he would not permit the old prison and lack of privilege for Wales, and had come to restore to everyone his possessions :

> Ni fyn y carchar a fu
> Neu gamraint fyth i Gymru.
> Yn enw Duw yna y daw
> I roddi i bawb yr eiddaw. (Cardiff MS. 48. p. 181.)

Unfortunately, the hopes of the nation were not to be fulfilled. Wales reckoned without the cold, crafty ambitious man who had used her to climb to a throne. Henry Tudor was no national leader, but simply a very ambitious man determined to rule over a large and strong kingdom. Wales was too small for him, and so was England. He had no intentions of ruling over two separate and distinct nations ; one of them must die. Unity to Henry, as to other rulers of his day meant uniformity. A strong kingdom must be homogeneous and he regarded it as imperative that Wales should cease to exist as a nation. It is true that Henry was kept too busy in England to carry out his intentions, but he passed them on as a settled policy towards Wales to his son and his son's children and to all the rulers of England henceforth. It is true that he tried, somewhat half-heartedly, to remove the more outstanding disabilities of the Welsh under the penal laws by granting them certain charters of liberty, but the English boroughs of North Wales, by their vigorous opposition, succeeded in having these attempts annulled. Strangely enough, dire as was the fate he intended for his own nation, Henry was proud, in his perverted way, of his Welsh blood, for he named his eldest son Arthur, and on his deathbed urged his son, Henry, to have a special memory for his own nation, the Welsh !

The bulk of the Welsh nation were so enraptured at the fulfilment of the prophecies that they were blinded to the true import of Tudor policy and accepted meekly at the hands of their beloved " Harri " and his descendants, treatment against which the whole nation would have risen had it been inflicted by an alien sovereign. All through Tudor times, Wales was pathetically convinced that her own rulers, so long foretold, would do nothing to harm her. Some few of the bards, however, noticed with dissatisfaction, that the millenium had not dawned for Wales, even though she had succeeded in placing the descendant of Cadwaladr on the throne of England. Lewis Glyn Cothi, that redoubtable old Nationalist, complains to Richard Herbert, constable of Aberystwyth, that life is still full of sorrow and the former bondage of those in bonds worse than ever. Llywelyn ap Hywel ab Ieuan ap Goronwy of Glamorgan is even more explicit, for he regards the splendid effort made by Wales on Henry's behalf as wasted effort. The Welsh, he says, are simply the servants of the men of Anglesey, Jasper and Harry, who prefer the men of the North (*i.e.* England) to those of their own nation :

> Gwae ni, daearu dirym
> Hil Gamber, mor ofer ym;
> Gwleddach ymhlith arglwyddi
> Gweision gan wŷr Môn ym ni. . . .
> Gwell gan Siaspar a Harri
> Y gwŷr o'r Nordd na'n gwŷr ni
> Ymddiried mae enaid Môn
> Eleni i'w elynion.

(Some 15th Century Bards of Glamorgan lxxxv.)

It was Henry VIII who carried out his father's wishes with regard to the nation he was to cherish so dearly in his Act of Union, 1536, and the other Acts relating to Wales passed during his reign. This Act has received much praise as an unmixed blessing to Wales, and no doubt some benefits did accrue from the Act, *e.g.* the Marcher Lordships, source of so much misery in the Middle Ages were abolished and turned into shire ground, one system of law was imposed upon all the inhabitants of Wales, English people in Wales were no longer to be highly privileged individuals, and Wales was given representation at Westminster. But it must be remembered that this Act was not a union of free and equal partners, but the engulfing of one by the other. This Act formally destroyed the separate existence of Wales and Henry VIII in all his legislation acted on the assumption that Wales was not a separate nation having its own characteristics and customs which must be respected, and having a language of its own. Tyrannous as Norman and English kings and officials had frequently been in the Middle Ages, the separate being of the Welsh people had never been denied. Now the Welshman, Henry VIII, denied the existence of the Welsh nation, made the English language the official language of Wales and no-one speaking Welsh only could hold office in his own country. He showed the same studied indifference to the historic territory of Wales, for in creating the new shires, land which belonged to Wales was incorporated in the English border counties. As Principal J. F. Rees has said : " the line between England and Wales could not be justified on geographical, historical, racial or linguistic grounds."

This is a policy which is still active, note the incorporation of Welsh Bicknor into England in the last century, Chester's attempt to take Saltney at the present time,—and of course, the attempt to take Monmouthshire. Tudor policy was to incorporate Wales in England by removing all the difference (on the Welsh side) between the two countries. Henceforth the Tudors and their successors have all behaved as though Wales was simply a part of England, and different in nothing—unless it is in being inferior to England in all things !

Their Welsh blood gave the Tudors an insight into the strength and weakness of the nation and how best to secure their policy of Anglicisation. The Welsh gentry, political leaders in the struggle for freedom and liberal patrons of Welsh culture, were made welcome at Court and enticed to London with offers of attractive careers. Here they gradually became Anglicised, and in the service of England their interest in their native land faded. This was a great blow to the bardic classes, who could not survive without noble patronage, and with their disappearance, a vigorous class of political nationalists, keenly watchful of their country's rights, disappeared. Instead of the bardic schools, English Grammar Schools were established to educate the children of the gentry on strictly English lines and rigidly excluding the Welsh language and Welsh culture. Knowledge of English became the avenue to wealth and fame and the Tudors did all in their power to bind the Welsh gentry to the Crown and alienate them from Wales. For the first time a rift appeared between the Welsh peasantry who remained Welsh and the Welsh gentry who became Anglicised, strangers in their own land. Strangely enough, Welsh literature in the period is completely silent on the question of the Act of Union, and there is very little evidence of the attitude of the Welsh towards any of the changes effected by Henry VIII. Probably, they were inclined to welcome the removal of the restrictions which had hampered them so long ; the arbitrary fixing of the Welsh boundary and the blow directed at the Welsh language were changes more apparent to posterity than to Tudor Wales. It is very unlikely that the nation desired the incorporation with England inaugurated by the Act ; the long fighting of the later Middle Ages which had carried the Tudor family to the throne of England had definitely been for the freedom of Wales, for the ideals of Owain Glyn Dŵr. The most likely reasons for Welsh acquiescence in Tudor policy must be found in the extraordinary, blind, worship of the Tudors by the Welsh nation, and the fact that, in securing the support of the gentry the Tudors had rendered the nation leaderless,—and a common people is generally easy to delude and slow to see the implications of political movements. Politically, the Tudors definitely established the course Wales was to take during the next four centuries and the Welsh people have submitted, almost without criticism during most of this period to the system which they established. During these centuries, the Tudors have been extremely popular in Wales, and their age regarded as the glorious era when Wales emerged from her mediaeval darkness into the light of modern civilisation and progress. We have had to wait until the present century before hearing a serious criticism of the Tudors and their behaviour towards Wales. Certainly the double tragedy of modern Wales has been that Owain Glyn Dŵr's Rising failed, and that, when she fulfilled the ancient prophecies in so remarkable a fashion, the leader whom she lifted to honour was unworthy of her trust. The Tudors left Wales no longer a nation, and the whole of the modern period has been the story of the slow and stubborn struggle of a poor and defenceless peasantry, scarcely conscious of the forces that impelled them or of the road which their feet instinctively trod " to become a nation once again".

Dr. CEINWEN THOMAS.

WALES A PART OF ENGLAND 1485—1800

HENRY Tudor's victory at Bosworth Field in 1485 was believed in Wales to be the fulfilment of prophecies which the bards had uttered through many generations of war and conquest. The new king was acclaimed as the *mab darogan*, the long-awaited liberator of his people. His landing in Wales had been heralded by an undertaking to deliver Welshmen from their " miserable servitudes," and his army, composed largely of Welshmen and marching under the banner of the Red Dragon, was deemed to have inflicted a national defeat on the English, and to have reversed the relationship between the two peoples. Thus, in Wales, the accession of the Tudor claimant to the English throne was regarded from a national standpoint. Henry had already announced four objectives for his campaign : first, to secure for himself his rightful possession, the Crown of England ; second, to overthrow the " odious tyrant," Richard III ; third, to restore the realm of England to its " ancient estate, honour and prosperity " ; and fourth, to regain for Welshmen their lawful rights and privileges, and to relieve them of the oppression under which they suffered. For the Welsh, the first three of these aims were overshadowed by the fourth. The penal laws of Henry IV had, in the fifteenth century, deprived Welshmen of the common rights of citizens, and reduced them to an outlawry which inflamed their nationalism anew. Throughout the whole of Welsh history the fifteenth century is the most bitterly anti-English. By 1485, indeed, the Welsh were in no mood to be satisfied with the mere restoration of their civic rights. At long last the " day of wrath " had arrived, the hour of vengeance for the sufferings of dire years of tyranny and suppression.

The events of 1485, too, lent some colour to the ancient claim that the Welsh, the descendants of the early Britons, were the rightful possessors not only of Wales but also of England. This view had lain in the subconsciousness of Welshmen for centuries, and had been frequently expressed by the bards. In the tenth century the author of *Armes Prydain Fawr* (The Prophecy of Great Britain) had urged an alliance of the Welsh and the Irish, the Vikings of Dublin and the men of Strathclyde and Brittany, to drive the English from the Island. Another prophesy in the Red Book of Hergest declared :

> It is certain that Owain will come,
> And conquer as far as London,
> And give joyful news to Welshmen.

The name " Owain " was applied by the bards at this period to the national deliverer whose arrival was eagerly awaited. After the failure of Glyndŵr's campaigns an unknown poet prophesied the rise of a second Owain who would come with "tumult" and "slaughter", and who in his anger would " burn as far as London", and on the eve of Henry Tudor's expedition yet another poet announced that the whole of Wales was ready to welcome him, " and to drive the descendants of Rhonwen headlong from this island". To those who believed in the prophecies it now appeared that their faith had been vindicated. The Crown of London was again worn by a Welshman of the race of Cadwaladr, and in Lewis Glyn Cothi's words : " the contemptuous wrath of the English has been of no avail, while all Welshmen are joyful".

Henry reigned for twenty-four years, but his policy showed little evidence of having been influenced by the ideas of the poets just quoted. An Italian who published a description of England in 1500 declared that the Welsh might " be said to have received their former independence, for the wise and fortunate Henry VII is a Welshman", but a contemporary poet in Wales, Llywelyn ap Hywel, composed a *cywydd* to complain of " Henry's neglect of the Welsh" and asserted that " Jasper and Henry prefer the men of the North to our men". Henry's principal care was the security of his throne and he gave scant attention to Welsh affairs. Yet in a number of secondary matters he found means of indicating his sense of indebtedness to the nation which had provided him with a path to the crown. A series of charters which he granted to certain towns and districts in North Wales extended specific privileges to their citizens, and many of the gentry who had supported his cause in 1485, such as Jasper Tudor, Sir Rhys ap Thomas and William Gruffydd of Penrhyn, were rewarded with office and advancement. By this means the administration of the affairs of Wales was entrusted to Welshmen, who were thereby provided with a solid interest in the permanency of the new dynasty. Henry asserted his Welsh descent publicly, flew the Welsh flag on appropriate occasions, and clothed the Welsh soldiers of his bodyguard in Welsh colours, white and green. He called his eldest son " Arthur," and sent him to hold court at Ludlow on the Welsh border. During his reign the Red Dragon was emblazoned on the Royal Coat-of-Arms and St. David's Day celebrated annually at Court.

The Tudor Government could not afford, however, to ignore Wales for too lengthy a period, and it was during the reign of Henry VIII (1509—47) that a comprehensive solution was sought for what might be described as the Welsh problem. For twenty-five years Henry took little interest in Wales, and while Sir Rhys ap Thomas lived, that is until 1526, the effective government of South Wales was entrusted entirely to him. Then, in 1534, Parliament began the enactment of a series of measures dealing specifically with conditions in Wales. The most important of these was the

Act of Union of 1536. The series was completed in 1542 by an Act defining and consolidating in detail, the provisions made in 1536. These statutes are the legislative corner-stone of modern Wales.

This "outburst" of Welsh legislation, as it has been called, was not something conceived in a vacuum and unrelated to contemporary events, but was rather a policy deliberately pursued in the face of danger and crises. Just as the Acts of 1707 and 1800, which united Scotland and Ireland with England, were war measures designed to serve the security of the realm of England, so Henry VIII's Welsh legislation of 1534—42 can only be understood against the general background of his conflict with the Papacy and the Catholic Powers of Europe. Henry had already married Anne Boleyn when Papal authority was abrogated in England in 1534 and 1535, and the dissolution of the lesser monasteries was begun in 1536. In 1534 the rebellion of Silken Thomas, son of the Earl of Kildare, had occurred in Ireland, and Henry saw his Continental enemies multiplying. Reports were coming in that the Irish were receiving aid, not only from Spain, but from Pembrokeshire in Wales, and that the allegiance of the Welsh troops in the king's service in Ireland was doubtful. There is evidence that sympathy with Queen Catherine was widespread in Wales at this time. In subsequent years, especially in 1539 and 1545, the Welsh coastal defences were strengthened against attack from the Continent. Particular attention was paid to Milford Haven, for Henry had not forgotten that this spot had been the scene of his father's landing in 1485, and of that of Glyndŵr's French allies in 1404.

The new Welsh policy can be seen beginning to take shape after 1526. In that year died Sir Rhys ap Thomas, the "King of Caeryw", of whom Rhys Nanmor said that

> The king owns the island,
> Except what belongs to Sir Rhys.

It was his decision to support Henry Tudor in 1485 that had turned the scales in the latter's favour in South Wales, and at no time was any attempt made to curtail his power or challenge his pre-eminence. His death at the age of 76 removed the last of the great mediaeval figures from the stage of Welsh public life.

Sir Rhys's heir was his young grandson, Sir Rhys ap Gruffydd, who has been described as a lover of books and solitude, with little personal ambition, and no taste for the life of the Court. Widespread astonishment was nevertheless aroused when it became known that not one of the high offices held by his grandfather was to be conferred upon him, and that an Englishman, Walter Devereux, Lord Ferrers, had been appointed Chief Justice and Chamberlain

of South Wales. In 1529, when Ferrers came to Carmarthen to
preside at his Court, some of his officials came into violent conflict
with Sir Rhys's tenants. A few days later Sir Rhys, supported by
a number of armed retainers, appeared in person before Carmarthen
castle and demanded the release of one of his servants from custody.
The affair ended with his own arrest and imprisonment in the
castle. A charge was subsequently brought against him in London
and the proceedings dragged on for two years. He was released
after the first hearing, then rearrested and confined to the Tower,
and released again. Ultimately he was accused of treason, found
guilty, and beheaded on December 4th, 1531. It appears that the
charge brought against him was one of plotting to cause an in-
surrection in Wales in support of James V of Scotland's designs on
the English Crown. The evidence adduced to sustain the
charge was flimsy, but weightier considerations than justice to
individuals were in the scale during those critical years of Henry
VIII's reign. After the execution of Sir Rhys ap Gruffydd, and
the forfeiture of his possessions, Henry could rest satisfied that
the most powerful family in Wales had been overthrown.

Politically, the condition of Wales at this time was one of disorder and confusion, even of chaos. There was no uniformity in
law or administration to provide a framework for the country's
historic unity of language and culture. The English shire system
was already established in the counties of Anglesey, Caernarvon,
Merioneth, Cardigan, Carmarthen and Flint, and its introduction
had commenced also in Glamorgan and Pembroke. The rest of
the country was still divided into Lordships of the March, territories which had been carved out of Wales by semi-independent
barons during the Norman aggression, and governed by them as
personal dominions. The effective independence of these lordships, it is true, was a thing of the past and many of them, including
some of the largest, had become Crown possessions. Nevertheless,
Wales had never been assimilated to the English political system,
and the king's writ had no authority in the courts of the Marcher
lordships. The shires were not represented at Westminster and
even the mediaeval Welsh law had not everywhere been entirely
superseded. In many districts neither Welsh nor English law was
effective and the rule of the outlaw persisted in the sturdy tradition
of the fifteenth century. It was possibly this latter factor that
gave the Government most immediate cause for anxiety and impelled it to energetic action.

The first step taken was the appointment of Bishop Rowland
Lee as President of the Council of the Marches in May, 1534. This
Council had been in existence since the previous century, but until
the bishop's appointment was a mere shadow. It was now transformed into an instrument fitted to bring the fear of the law to the

farthest reaches of the land. In 1532 Sir Edward Croft, one of its officials, complaining that Wales was "far out of order" and that many murderers escaped unpunished for their crimes, had urged that "some man . . . . be sent down to us to use the sword of justice where he shall see cause, throughout the Principality. Otherwise the Welsh will wax so wild, it will not be easy to bring them to order again". Rowland Lee's commission to Wales was Thomas Cromwell's answer to this request.

Lee was described by one of Cromwell's spies as "an earthly beast, a mole, and an enemy to all godly learning into the office of his damnation—a papist, an idolater, and a fleshly priest". Another observer testified that he was "not affable to any of the Walshrie". Undismayed by bloodshed he was a born pursuer of men, more at ease in the horseman's habit than the priestly garb, and for nine years, till his death in 1543, he pitilessly hunted the felons and outlaws of Wales and the March. His operations were facilitated from the outset by the enactment during the three years 1534—6 of a series of laws of which one aimed at preventing the escape of offenders from Wales to the Forest of Dean or across the Severn, while another empowered the President of the Council of the Marches to punish jurymen who brought in verdicts contrary to the evidence. The bearing of arms and the holding of *cymhorthau* were also prohibited, and power given to officials in English counties to prosecute for offences committed in the Marcher Lordships.

Who were these offenders whom the bishop pursued so relentlessly to the scaffold? In his view they were all merely thieves and highway robbers. The historian should note, however, that a life of "outlawry" was deemed honourable in Wales since the war of Owain Glyndŵr and that many had chosen the freedom of the woodlands rather than submit to the Englishry of the towns. In the fifteenth century poets composed *cywyddau* in praise of the outlaws. Thus Tudur Penllyn addressed the celebrated Dafydd ap Siancyn with the words, "thy castle is the woodland, thy towers are the oaks of the meadow", adding that however desirable the shelter of the town might be, "better the ravine and the grey crags!" Another poet, Llywelyn ap y Moel, who had himself been an outlaw, claimed that "to capture an Englishman and seize his accoutrements" beneath Coed y Graig Lwyd was a much more profitable undertaking than the ancient custom of presenting the gentry with eulogies in expectation of largesse. A century separated these spacious days from those of Rowland Lee, and it is difficult to tell to what extent the patriotic motive persisted in 1534. But it should not be forgotten that the habit of living without the law was born of the conflict of two peoples, conquerors and conquered. As a class the outlaws had inherited a tradition that they were men fighting for their land and freedom, and it is improbable that this view had been totally obliterated even though two Tudors had occupied the throne of England.

Pacification by sword and scaffold were, however, merely the first steps of the settlement which Henry and Cromwell envisaged for Wales. In due time Rowland Lee was made to understand that the scourge he wielded was only the harsh prelude to a subtler and more pliant policy, which he could neither commend nor support. The new orientation was announced in the Act of Union of 1536 and was doubtless the fruit of long meditation on the king's part. Its germ may be seen in a letter on Irish affairs which Henry wrote to Lord Surrey in 1520, in which, having declared his despair of ever being able to reduce the Irish lords by war and violence, he expressed the hope of winning their co-operation and allegiance " by sober ways, politic drifts, and amiable persuasions, founded in law and reason, rather than by rigorous dealing".[1] Treated thus, Henry argued, they could be led to identify their interests with his. This was the policy proposed for Wales by the Act of Union. In Ireland it failed, but in Wales, where it could be firmly founded on the national regard for the Welsh origin of the Tudors, its success was so overwhelming that its nature and fruits are only today being fully understood.

The purpose and intention of the Act is thus set forth in the preamble:

. . . . . . by cause that in the same Countrey, Principalitie and dominion dyvers rights, usages, laws and customes be farre discrepant frome the lawes and customes of this Realme; and also by cause that the people of the same dominion have and do daily use a speche nothing like ne consonaunt to the naturall mother tonge used within this Realme, some rude and ignorant people have made distinccion and diversitie betwene the Kinges Subiectes of this Realme and hys subiectes of the said dominion and Principalitie of Wales, whereby greate discorde, variaunce, debate, dyvysion, murmer and sedicion hath growen betwene his said subiectes; his highnes, therefore, of a singuler love and favour that he beareth towardes his subiectes of his said dominion of Wales, mynding, and entending to reduce them to the perfecte order, notice and knowlege of the lawes of this his Realme and utterly to extirpe alle and singuler the sinister usages and customes differinge frome the same, and to bring his said subiectes of this his Realme and of his said dominion of Wales to an amiable concorde and unitie, hath . . . . . .ordeyned, enacted and establsshed that his said

---
1. *State Papers, Henry VIII*, II, 52; cf. Eleanor Hull, *A History of Ireland*, i, 289.

countrey or dominion of Wales shalbe stonde and contynue for ever fromehensforthe incorporated, united and annexed to and with his Realme of Englande.[2]

The passage needs no elucidation. The country referred to as "this Realme" is, of course, England, and the purport of the Act was to extend to Welshmen all the privileges and obligations of English citizenship. In return, the Welsh were required to renounce their nationality and separate political identity. Wales was summarily bid to reject her past, disclaim her distinctive character, and acquiesce in absorption by England.

The Act therefore decreed that English was to be the sole official language of all legal and government business in Wales. A Welshman who was ignorant of English was thereby disqualified from holding any public office in his own country. The Welsh system of land inheritance by equal division, known as *gavelkind*, was to be discontinued and replaced by the English system of primogeniture. Out of the Marcher lordships the five new shires of Denbigh, Montgomery, Radnor, Brecknock and Monmouth were created, and other portions of Marcher territory were added to the English counties of Shropshire, Herefordshire and Gloucestershire. The boundaries of Pembrokeshire and Glamorgan were extended and Parliamentary representation at Westminster granted to the Welsh counties and county boroughs. The border between Wales and England was not drawn according to any national line of demarcation and districts which were Welsh in tradition and speech, such as Ewyas Lacy and Oswestry, were excluded from Wales. Two commissions were appointed by the Act with instructions to report on the implementation of its provisions. By 1542 their labours were complete and that year's final enactment, defining such matters as shire boundaries in minute detail, set the seal on Henry VIII's Welsh policy. The Welsh problem, it was believed, was now solved, and the country would settle down and accommodate itself to the status of a collection of English counties. Legally the Welshman was an Englishman, and Wales incorporated into England.

The realities of nature and history, however, could not be ignored or brushed aside so easily. The assimilation of Wales to England has never been made final and absolute, and it has at no time been possible to govern the two countries on the assumption that no distinction of any kind existed between them. Even the Acts of Union in some measure acknowledged the distinctiveness of Wales by establishing a Chancery and an Exchequer at Denbigh and at Brecon, modelled on those already existing at Caernarvon,

---

2. The text of the Act of Union is given by William Rees, *The Union of England and Wales*, 81—100.

and by the institution of the Courts of Great Sessions to adminster English law in Wales. It was stated in the Act of 1536 that the creation of local institutions was necessary because of the expense and inconvenience to litigants involved in a journey from Wales to the London courts. Accordingly the Act of 1542 provided for the holding of courts twice annually in each of the Welsh counties, except Monmouthshire, by the Justices of the Great Sessions. This system continued until its abolition in 1830. Monmouthshire, however, was detached for juridical purposes from the rest of Wales and subjected to the jurisdiction of the Westminster courts. It is notorious that this provision has for centuries been quoted to sustain the claim, contrary to all the evidence of history and affinity, that Monmouthshire is an English county. In addition to the establishment of the Courts of Great Sessions, the authority of the Council of the Marches, with its Court at Ludlow, was confirmed and extended. This Council, originally created in the fifteenth century, continued to function until 1689 apart from a period of abeyance during the Civil War and Protectorate. It was subject to the direction of the Privy Council and exercised authority throughout the thirteen Welsh counties and the four English counties of Shropshire, Herefordshire, Worcestershire and Gloucestershire. It will thus be seen that, in spite of the Tudor Government's desire to remove every feature which distinguished Wales from England, in administrative practice this did not prove feasible at the time.

Unlike the later Acts of Union of 1707 and 1800, which respectively united the national parliaments of Scotland and Ireland with that of England, the Act of 1536 did not abolish a Welsh Parliament. The Norman and Edwardian conquest had denied Wales the possibility of developing parliamentary institutions, and by 1536 her people had long been familiar with English administrators and officials. In large tracts of the country the English laws of inheritance had already supplanted the ancient Welsh custom. In one sense the Act of 1536 was merely the completion of a process which had been manifest locally and intermittently for centuries.

Even so the purpose of the first of the Acts of Union, as of those that followed it, was to bring about uniformity within the realm. Impelled by what appeared to them to be political and military necessity, its promoters believed that a state uniform in speech and religion would be better equipped to meet the threat of foreign aggression. Another and quite different factor which influenced them was the prevailing view of cultural values. By this time the manners of London Society had come to be regarded as the standard of civilisation, and the language of culture, in Britain and Ireland at least, was considered to be English. This attitude is well illustrated by the reference in the Act of Union to " the sinister usages and customes " which still persisted in Wales. The lack during these centuries of a Welsh capital city, acting as a focus for the national culture, was an irreparable loss. English writers of the period frequently used the word ' civilitie ', meaning thereby the qualities of urbanity and gentility of which London was, in their view, the obvious centre and source. Among the educated classes it was believed that this metropolitan virtue could be transplanted to Wales and, with tender nurture and a modicum of faith, made to blossom amid the quarrelsome squires and mountain farmers. Sir John Wynne of Gwedir, describing the thriving state of trade and the prosperity of the legal profession at Caernarvon, remarks that

> Civility and learning flourished in that towne, soe as they were called the lawyers of Carnarvon, the merchands of Beaumares and the gentlemen of Conway.

At best this was only an aping of the manners of English urban life. In England the century following the Act of Union witnessed the flowering of the English Renaissance in the works of Spenser and Sidney, Marlowe and Shakespeare and Jonson, but in Wales, where the last of the great *cywyddwyr* were composing their last eulogies and elegies and the entire mediaeval culture was in decay, the new culture of the Renaissance was denied an opportunity of fully expressing itself in a Welsh garb.

For the Welsh gentry heartily and unanimously welcomed the Tudor new order. To them as a class it brought advancement and increased wealth. London now became for a numerous section of them a centre of activity and a focus of interests, and for the remainder a source of social and cultural standards. Mr. Saunders Lewis has shown how the change in the tone of Welsh aristocratic society is reflected in the *cywyddau* of Tudur Aled, whom he describes as " the poet of the new Welsh courtier-class, composed of men whose only ambition was a career and the acquirement of wealth". In his *Life and Reign of King Henry the Eighth*, Lord Herbert of Cherbury, (1581—1648) relates that before 1536 certain of the Welsh gentry had petitioned King Henry to unite Wales with England. The address which they sent him opened with the words:

> We, on the part of your highness's subjects, inhabiting that portion of the island which our invaders first called Wales, most humbly prostrate at your highness's feet, do crave to be received and adopted into the same laws and privileges which your other subjects enjoy: neither shall it hinder us (we hope) that we have liv'd so long under our own.... We.... do here voluntarily resign, and humble our selves to that sovereignty, which we acknowledge so well invested in your highness. Nor is this the first time; we have always attended an occasion to unite our selves to the greater and better parts of the island.

The Union itself was welcomed and applauded by every member of the Welsh upper class who expressed an opinion thereon. Such writers as William Salesbury and Humfrey Llwyd declared that Wales had been liberated from slavery and oppression and granted equality with England. The view of Dr. David Powel was that nothing so beneficial had ever happened to the common people of Wales as the Union, and according to George Owen of Henllys, the government of Wales had been " reformed " during Henry VIII's reign and " sweete and wholesome Lawes " provided for the land. When the union of Scotland and England was being canvassed during the reign of James I, reference was frequently made to the precedent which had proved so successful in Wales. The crowning paean of praise was uttered by Edmund Burke in a glowing passage of his famous speech on Conciliation with the American Colonies, ending with the words :

> From that moment, as by a charm, the tumults subsided, obedience was restored ; peace, order and civilisation followed in the train of liberty. When the day-star of the English constitution had arisen in their hearts, all was harmony, within and without.

Indeed, the only important critic of the Act of Union was Bishop Rowland Lee. He, however, was a survival from the fifteenth century, and he failed to sense the subtlety and flexibility of the Tudor policy. In his view to appoint Welshmen as justices of the peace would be merely to invite felons to judge felons. " For thieves I found them", he declared in 1537, " and thieves I shall leave them".

One outside observer differed from contemporary Welshmen in his assessment of the situation. Chapuys, the ambassador of the Emperor Charles V in London, wrote in 1534, at an early stage of Henry VIII's Welsh legislation :

> The distress of the people is incredible, especially the Welsh, from whom, by Act of Parliament, the King has just taken away their native laws, customs and privileges, which is the very thing they can endure least patiently. I wonder how the king dared do it during these troubles in Ireland, except that God wishes so to blind him.

He reported also that the Welsh were aiding the rebellion in Ireland and refusing to enlist in the English forces raised to suppress the Irish. Chapuys's opinion, however, was coloured by his own desires. He failed to comprehend the peculiar background and character of the Welsh attachment to the Tudors, and did not realise that the accession of this family to the throne had, in the main, reversed a policy of repression and opened a new period of unprecedented personal advancement and gratification of ambition for the Welsh gentry. The new opportunities offered to the latter were sufficient compensation, in their view, for any temporary inconveniences the Tudor policy might occasion. By this time the idea of a separate Welsh state had been lost, and the ancient political and legal institutions of Wales replaced by a " Welsh " king "adorned with the Crown of London."

Thus a millenium of Welsh history came to an end. A division now appeared in the national life, an ever-widening breach separating the gentry from the common people. The crystallisation of landlordism into a social system and the anglicisation of the upper classes proceeded simultaneously. Becoming increasingly alienated from its traditions and heritage, the Welsh aristocratic class renounced the duties and obligations which for time out of mind it had discharged and honoured. The change, though gradual, was completed by the end of the eighteenth century. It is this defection of the aristocracy, and its withdrawal from the stage of Welsh national life, that gives unity to the period we are discussing. The common people were left to toil unremittingly, not merely for their own bare sustenance, but for the maintenance of a propertied class which was discarding all sense of responsibility for the well-being of a native Welsh society. From that period till today the main theme of Welsh history has been the effort of the people to recreate a society and to raise up new leaders to take the place of those who had deserted them. A general awakening did not occur until the eighteenth century, and its early manifestations were religious and educational in character. The rebirth of a political national consciousness was delayed till the nineteenth century.

The changes of the Tudor period are reflected in the works of some of the later *cywydd* poets. These do not mention the Act of Union itself but refer frequently to the social effects of the new policy. For instance, Siôn Tudur bitterly attacks the greed of the new landlords and the insolence of the new-rich merchant class who affected the station of gentry, the growth of usury, the prevalence of corruption among officials and justices, and the servility of poets who addressed their eulogies to the unworthy and " gave extravagant genealogies to every Tom, Dick and Harry". The decline of patronage and the degradation of the bardic order is lamented in the following words by Simwnt Fychan :—

> In former times poets were joyfully maintained by generous patrons, receiving worthy praise and ready respect, apparel of silk, fitting honours, gold and true affection; today, whatever their merit, they receive neither honour nor affection, nor wealth, nor respect, nor profit, nor dignity, nor ready sustenance, nor increase of possessions, nor apparel. . . . . .[3]

---

3. Gwenogvryn Evans, *Reports on Welsh MSS.* I, 250.

The traditional qualities of the Welsh gentry did not, of course, disappear overnight. Much litigation was caused by the effort and strain involved in fitting Welsh society into an English legal framework, and innumerable local disputes and family feuds are recorded in such sources as the Star Chamber Proceedings and the Wynn Papers. Discussing the latter Professor A. H. Dodd observes:

> The abiding impression..... is that, till late in the seventeenth century at least, English party labels were but a veneer in Wales; the blood-tie and the blood-feud were the solid realities.[4]

It would at present be premature to attempt to write the political history of this period, the documentary materials of which still await much research and interpretation. The State Papers for 1598—9 contain the intriguing statement that five hundred Welshmen served under Hugh O'Neill, Earl of Tyrone in Ireland, during his campaign against the English.[5] The report affirms that the Welshmen believed that Tyrone was a descendant of Owain Glyndŵr, that he had friends in Wales and had been proclaimed Prince of Wales, and that Tyrone was a Welsh name, " Tir Owain". What basis there was for this report, who these Welshmen were and what was their motive, is not known. It is, however, known that the forces which accompanied the Earl of Essex to Ireland on his ill-starred expedition against Tyrone in 1599 included a number of Welshmen, in spite of a warning contained in the above-mentioned report that Welshmen could not be trusted to fight against the Irish. There is also preserved among the State Papers a manuscript book, dedicated to Essex, which purports to set forth reasons why Ireland should be kept in perpetual subjection to England. It describes Ireland as the back-armour of England, and adds the following enigmatic observation:

> It is very certain that, if that back part of the armour should miscarry, and be cut off from England (as God forbid it should) it would make the old brutes of Wales to look about them more than they do now.[6]

In 1601 the Earl of Essex, aiming at regaining his former influence in Government circles and pre-eminence at Court, committed himself to an act of armed rebellion in London. He possessed extensive estates in South-West Wales, and his following included a not inconsiderable percentage of Welshmen, led by Sir Gelly Meyrick. A band of Welsh gentry, riding to London to aid him, was only persuaded to discontinue the journey by the news of the failure of the rebellion. Bishop David Mathew in *The Celtic*

---

4. *Arch. Camb.* 1927, p. 204.
5. *Cal. State Papers (Irish)*, 1598—9, p. 462.
6. *Ibid.*, 507.

Peoples and Renaissance Europe, maintains that the Welsh squires looked to the Devereux, Earls of Essex, for protection for themselves and their ancient customs against the encroachment of the officials of the Council of the Marches at Ludlow. In this incident, he claims, may be discerned the last manifestation of the national spirit of the old Welsh aristocracy, the last occasion on which the Welsh squires united " to support a private citizen to assist their own nation with arms".[7] Thereafter English government of Wales was " perfectly effective". Within half a century the sons and grandsons of these squires would again ride forth to battle, but this time, in a vain but absolute loyalty, to defend King Charles I of England against enemies sprung from his own people.

Complaints against the Council of the Marches at Ludlow were frequent. It was accused of corruption, partisanship, profiteering, delay, negligence and waste. Yet, while it lasted, it was at least an acknowledgement of the distinctiveness of Wales. Its most distinguished President was Sir Henry Sidney (1559—86). For a long period Ludlow was the political, though not the cultural, capital of Wales, and its Norman castle was familiar with scenes of regal pomp and ceremony. It was there in 1634 that Milton's *Comus* was performed, in which Wales was saluted, with unconscious irony, as

> An old and haughty nation, proud in arms.

The Council was also an object of criticism on account of the inclusion of four English counties, Shropshire, Herefordshire, Gloucestershire and Worcestershire, within the area of its jurisdiction. During the reign of James I there was a long and energetic campaign for the termination of its authority in these counties, but the king, choosing to regard this demand as an attack on the prerogative, set his face against any change. It was also argued that to confine the Council's jurisdiction to Wales would arouse contempt for the Welsh among the English and " ere longe revive the auncient enmytie betweene those two people and bring all to the old confusion againe".[8] The Council's fate was sealed when the Long Parliament met in 1640. In the following year its jurisdiction was terminated, except in civil actions, and for twenty years it ceased to function. When the Monarchy was restored in 1660 it was reestablished as a court for civil pleas, but was finally abolished in 1689, after the accession of William and Mary. Thereafter there remained only one institution, the Courts of Great Sessions, which formally recognised Wales as a nation.

---

7. Mathew, 456.
8. Skeel, *The Council in the Marches of Wales*, 136.

The history of the early Welsh members of Parliament, up to 1642, has been written by Professor A. H. Dodd[9]. They did not find their feet immediately, but in the course of time a few of their number, such as Sir John Perrot, came to play a prominent part in the general business of Parliament. They were usually Welshmen of the land-owning class, though occasionally an Englishman was found in their ranks. Matters concerning Wales and local affairs in Wales frequently engaged the attention of Parliament. The most amusing of the Welsh Members of this period was Sir William Maurice of Clenennau, grandfather of the better-known Sir John Owen. Described as "the complete Tudor Welshman", this worthy gentleman always vigorously asserted his nationality but nevertheless never tired of extolling the Union with England. Over forty of his speeches are recorded. Their unfailing subject was the improvement in the condition of Wales brought about by the Union, and the desirability of uniting Scotland with England in similar fashion. His orations were long and boring and burdened with innumerable references to Welsh history and frequently moved the compiler of the *Journals* of the House to such acid comments as " a long unnecessarie speech", or " an Idle speech. . . . .which moved laughter in the House". So tiresome did the English members find him that one of them turned on him on one occasion with the charge that the Welsh were a nation of Devil-worshippers and " the most base, pesantly, perfidious people of the World". Serenely impervious to the displeasure of the English members, however, Sir William's loyalty never wavered. During the controversy concerning the demand for the termination of the jurisdiction of the Council of the Marches in the four English border counties he urged its continuance on the ground that these counties had been included with Wales in order to strengthen the hands of the President of the Council against the "rudeness" of the rebellious Welsh.

On the Union of the English and Scottish crowns in 1603 the Red Dragon had been removed from the Royal Court-of-Arms and replaced by the Unicorn of Scotland. The Stuarts were no believers in Welsh nationality. James I aimed at the union not only of the crowns but of the parliaments of England and Scotland, and in one of his speeches referred to " the maturity of time, which must piece and piece take away the distinction of nations as it hath already done here between England and Wales".[10] By this time the allegiance of the Welsh squires was firmly established and during the Civil War Wales almost unanimously supported King Charles. The country possessed no urban merchant class which could provide favourable soil for the growth of anti-royalist sentiment. Charles recruited a substantial portion of his forces from Wales,

9. *Transactions of the Cymmrodorion Society*, 1942 ; 1945 ; 1946—7.
10. *Cal. of Hatfield MSS.*, XVI, 364.

although his cause was somewhat embarrassed by his officers' ignorance of the Welsh language and their disrespect for local tradition. The Parliamentary pamphleteers treated Welshmen in general as objects of ridicule and ascribed to them every imaginable shortcoming, including cowardice, ignorance, superstition, faulty English, excessive pride of lineage and an insatiable appetite for leeks and toasted cheese. One pamphlet, *The Parliament Explained to Wales* (1640), written by a Welshman, John Lewis of Llanbadarn Fawr, displays an exceptional standpoint which Mr. Myrddin Lloyd has described as " messianic nationalism".[11] Its author points out " how the Lord hath so marvellously preserved our Tongue " and declares his belief that Divine Providence has reserved an especial task for the Welsh nation to fulfil at some future date. The Puritan Government, however, regarded Wales as a land shrouded in darkness and a field for missionary activity, as is shown by the " Act for the Propagation of the Gospel in Wales " which passed through Parliament in 1650.

While during this period the consciousness of nationality in Wales greatly declined and abated, it was in some measure sustained by the prose writers whose work filled the gap in Welsh Literature left by the decay of the bardic system and whose significance as a movement was first appraised by Emrys ap Iwan in his essay *Y Clasuron Cymraeg*. Though the majority of their works were translations from other languages into Welsh, some of them exhibit superb mastery of Welsh prose. The Welsh version of the Bible was the most important task undertaken, and it is beyond doubt that the survival of Welsh as a living speech to modern times is primarily due to the influence of that magnificent work. It should be noted, however, that the translators were usually impelled by religious rather than patriotic or literary motives. They acquiesced in the official view that "to attain uniformity of speech among the inhabitants of the same island was an end to be greatly desired", but nevertheless believed that an even more urgent need was to render the Gospel immediately accessible to Welshmen in a language which they understood. The service they did to the Welsh language was incidental rather than intentional.

Contemporary with the translators were the scholars and grammarians, such as Dr. John Davies of Mallwyd, Dr. Siôn Dafydd Rhys and the exiled Dr. Gruffydd Robert of Milan. These men believed in the intrinsic value of the Welsh language and of Welsh culture and their work constitutes a link in the faint continuity of Welsh national consciousness from its decline in the early postmediaeval period to the first stirrings of its revival in the eighteenth

---

11. D. Myrddin Lloyd, *Cenedlaetholdeb a Rhyfel* (Pamffledi Heddychwyr Cymru), 17.

century. " He who denies his father and mother, his country and his language", said Gruffydd Robert, " will never be gentle or virtuous". The same period witnessed the birth of the Antiquarian Movement. This movement, however, was too frequently animated by an interest in the Welsh past as a dead relic rather than as the history of a living nation. For many of the Welsh historians of this time Welsh history had ended in 1282, or at the latest with Henry Tudor's accession in 1485. Mention must nevertheless be made of one of the antiquarians, Robert Vaughan of Hengwrt (1592—1667), for the outstanding collection of manuscripts which he accumulated became one of the indispensable foundation-stones of modern Welsh scholarship.

Among the masters of Welsh prose in the seventeenth century was Morgan Llwyd, but his political thought and viewpoint were not Welsh. On the other hand Charles Edwards adopted an undeniably national and patriotic attitude in his *Hanes y Ffydd Ddiffuant*, particularly in his treatment of the Welsh princes, but even he adds that the rebellion of Owain Glyndŵr was harmful to Wales because it was the occasion of the penal legislation of Henry IV. He lavishes praise on Henry VIII for extending to Welshmen " the same privileges, freedom and justice " as the English enjoyed, and declares further: " The English, who formerly were ravenous wolves, have for us become cherishing shepherds. . . . . England is open to us too and we are as free to live there unmolested as our ancestors before they lost it". The English were in fact less cherishing than Charles Edwards imagined. Anti-Welsh pamphlets continued to flow from the press in England even after the end of the Civil War. A notorious specimen is *Wallography* (1682), which thus passes judgment on the Welsh language.

> Their native gibberish is usually prattled throughout the whole of Taphydom except in their market towns, whose inhabitants being a little raised do begin to despise it. 'Tis usually cashiered out of gentlemen's houses. . . . .so that (if the stars prove lucky) there may be some glimmering hopes that the British language may be quite extinct and may be English'd out of Wales.[12]

Another pamphlet considered that Welsh was " inarticulate and gutteral and sounds more like the gobbling of geese or turkeys than the speech of rational creatures". Having been deprived of social status and prestige the language was becoming increasingly an object of contempt, and by the eighteenth century, though still used by writers of the calibre of Ellis Wynne and Theophilus Evans, its speedy disappearance was expected by many.

---

12. W. J. Hughes, *Wales and the Welsh in English Literature*, 45.

In 1746 Parliament enacted that in all legislation the word "England" was to be understood as including Wales. That the absorption of Wales by England had been completed was obviously the prevailing view. The date was too early for the significance of the characteristic movements of the eighteenth century, then in their incipient stages and later to shape and dominate Welsh life, to be apparent. It was only a bare decade since Gruffydd Jones of Llanddowror had set his system of circulating schools in motion, and the leaders of the Methodist Revival had begun preaching and establishing *seiadau*. Neither of these movements was interested in Welsh nationality or in the Welsh language as such, but their ultimate influence on the fate of both was profound. Apart from their purely religious effect they created an intellectual awakening among the common people, made them literate, and provided a reading public for the books and periodicals which issued from the press in increasing numbers at the end of the eighteenth and throughout the nineteenth centuries. They liberated the latent energies of the Welsh people, and the political movements of the nineteenth century were in very large measure their indirect results. It is, nevertheless, in the classical literary movement led by the Morrises of Anglesey, Goronwy Owen and Ieuan Fardd that the germ of a new Welsh national consciousness may be discerned. The founding of the Cymmrodorion Society in London in 1751, one of the rare national acts of the eighteenth century, was among the fruits of this movement. The aims of the Cymmrodorion included not only the patronage of Welsh literature and learning, but also the promotion of trade and industry in Wales in order to provide employment for Welshmen in their own country. In their political ideas, of course, the leaders of the movement were subject to the limitations of their time. The Morris brothers were civil servants who had no quarrel with the State. Goronwy Owen had no conception of Welsh national unity and described his fellow-countrymen of South Wales as "only half Welshmen," and their speech as "disgusting" and "barbarous". Ieuan Fardd also praised the Tudors for delivering Wales from the English oppression:—

> The English galling yoke they took away,
> And govern'd Britons with the mildest sway.[13]

Nevertheless, this small circle of writers was the fountain-head of modern Welsh nationalism. Here were men with a consciousness of their nationality founded on a knowledge of Welsh history, a burning enthusiasm for Welsh literature, and a pride in their entire cultural inheritance. Goronwy Owen's letters are full of this spirit, but national sentiment was most ardent in Ieuan Fardd. In his bitter *cywydd*, *Hiraeth y Bardd am ei Wlad* (The Poet's Longing for his Country), the latter describes his journey "to Kent, to the odious

. D. Silvan Evans, *Gwaith y Parchedig Evan Evans*, 143.

atmosphere of the English, dreary wretches," where he pined amid "inhospitable churls". His elegy on the death of William Vaughan of Corsygedol shows that, in spite of his admiration for the Tudors, he had perceived the tragedy of the ancient Welsh aristocracy :

> To the gluttonous great ones of our land
> Corruption came from England ;
> . . . .
> Upon them and their children their choice
> Has brought a curse, and oblivion.

But his nationalism expressed itself most forcibly when he condemned the contemporary policy, consistently and rigorously pursued, of appointing Englishmen of anti-Welsh views to occupy the Welsh episcopal sees. Ieuan Fardd, though only a poor curate without hope of preferment, was a Welsh scholar unrivalled in his generation. It embittered him beyond words to see that the Church he served was being deliberately used as an instrument of Anglicisation in Wales. "As Bishops," he said " we have only worthless grasping self-seekers, who endeavour to deprive us of the light of God's Word in our own language." Elsewhere he adds that " our Bishops look upon me, I believe in my conscience, with an evil eye because I dare have any affection for my country, language, and antiquities, which in their opinion, had better been lost and forgotten"[14]

There were occasions when these bishops appointed monoglot English clergymen to livings in Welsh-speaking districts of Wales. Once, at least, this policy was publicly challenged. When a certain Dr. Bowles, an Englishman, was granted the living of Trefdraeth in Anglesey proceedings were taken against him in the Court of Arches in London, by the churchwardens of Trefdraeth, with the help and support of the Cymmrodorion Society. The court rejected a plea for his removal from Trefdraeth, but expressed the opinion that such appointments should not in future be made. The most revealing aspect of the case was the argument of counsel for the defendant, which ran as follows :—

> Wales is a conquered country, it is proper to introduce the English language, and it is the duty of the bishops to endeavour to promote the English, in order to introduce the lanuage. . . . . . .It has always been the policy of the legislature to introduce the English language into Wales. We never heard of an act of parliament in Welsh. . . . . .The English language is, by act of parliament, to be used in all the courts of judicature

---

14. *Ibid.*, 201, 182.

in Wales, and an English Bible to be kept in all the churches in Wales, that by comparison of that with the Welsh, they may the sooner attain to the knowledge of the English.[15]

There we have an uncompromising restatement of Tudor policy. The Welsh language was regarded as an abomination and no Act of Parliament acknowledged its legal existence between 1662 and 1836.

One incident however is recorded, before the end of the eighteenth century, in which the consciousness of Welsh nationality became effective even in the political field. In 1780 Edmund Burke announced his intention of bringing a series of measures before Parliament for the reform of certain institutions of the state. One of these would have the effect of reducing the number of the justices of the Great Sessions in Wales from eight to three, and its purpose was described as " the more perfectly uniting to the Crown the Principality of Wales and the County Palatine of Chester and for the more commodious administration of justice within the same." Later in 1782, Burke withdrew this measure and explained his action in the following statement:

> Care had been taken to poison the minds of the Welch, and to fill them with an idea, that the intended reform was in reality meant as an attack upon the principality: the Welch were full of this idea; and as long as they were prepossessed with it, he would not force his reform upon them against their will; he would wait till time and better information should have wrought a change in their opinion.[16]

A strong case could undoubtedly be made for this particular reform, which Burke had originally proposed as a part of his campaign against public waste and corruption. It should be remembered too that the Courts of Great Sessions had at no time given any encouragement to the use of the Welsh language. Of the 217 judges who during 288 years dispensed justice from their benches not more than 30 were natives of Wales, and of these it is improbable that more than a fraction could speak Welsh. Yet, in 1780 this was the only institution of the realm which formally recognised Wales as a nation. For a country deprived of freedom any institution of state which is national in form, however subordinate and imperfect it may be, has an exceptional value. It is clear that there were some in Wales in 1780—82 who, perhaps unconsciously, took this view.

---

15. *The Depositions, Arguments and Judgment in the Cause of The Churchwardens of Trefdraeth, in the County of Anglesey, Against Dr. Bowles*. Published by the Society of Cymmrodorion, London, MDCCLXXIII, p. 59.
16. *Parliamentary Debates*, 1782, p. 126.

Less than ten years later the French Revolution burst upon Europe. It was an event which inspired and profoundly influenced many national movements. In Ireland it implanted the germ of the demand for an independent republic. In Wales on the other hand, where the political sense of nationality was shallow and rudimentary, its effect was different. Although some of the handful of Welshmen who welcomed the Revolution advocated the public and official use of the Welsh language, their political aim was democracy in Britain as a whole. Their activities were nevertheless an important contribution to the new orientations which appeared in Wales in the nineteenth century.

A. O. H. JARMAN.

NATIONAL MOVEMENTS IN WALES IN THE NINETEENTH CENTURY.

THE history of the nineteenth century in Wales can be divided into three periods : (1) 1801—1850, (II) 1850—1880 ; (III) 1880—1900 :

(I) 1801—1850.

The abolition of the Courts of Great Sessions, and the publication of the Reports of the Commissioners of Inquiry into the State of Education in Wales were the two main events in the history of Welsh movements of a national character during the first half of the last century.

The history of the Great Sessions has been written by W. R. Williams in *The Great Sessions in Wales and the Welsh Judges, 1542—1830*, and is also to be found in *The Welsh People* by John Rhys and D. Brynmor Jones, (pp. 377—394), *A Making of Modern Wales* by Howell T. Evans, (pp. 158—162) *Modern Welsh History*, by Idris Jones, (pp. 32—36) and in an article entitled " The King's Court of Great Sessions in Wales", by W. Llewelyn Williams, which was first published in *Y Cymmrodor*, vol. XXVI, and afterwards included, with but few alterations in his book, *The Making of Modern Wales* (pp. 128—194). The last mentioned is the best study on the history of the Great Sessions yet to appear, although comparatively little space is given in it to the abolition of the Courts. It requires legal minds like those of Brynmor Jones and Llewelyn Williams to deal with the Courts of Great Sessions as a judicature whereas our aim, in turning to the volumes of Hansard and the periodicals and newspapers of that day, is to discover the opinions prevalent in Wales, and amongst her M.P's, on the abolition.

Edmund Burke was the first to advocate this step.[1] In his speech in the House of Commons, February 11, 1780, he made two points regarding Wales. (1) The authority of the king did not extend over the whole of Britain. The king ruled in England only ; the county palatine of Chester was under the authority of the Earl, Cornwall under the Duke, Lancashire likewise, and Wales was under the authority of her Prince. Britain consisted of England and five provinces, and the latter were not under the direct authority of the king of England. It was ridiculous that they should be independent in law and finance. Not only did they have their own separate

---

1. *The Speeches of the Right Honourable Edmund Burke, in The House of Commons, and in Westminster-Hall. In Four Volumes.* The title of the speech in question is " Mr. Burke's Plan of Economical Reform". The references to Wales are found from page 29 to 37 in the second volume.

judicature, but they also had their own treasuries. Burke followed Lord Coke in his view that there was a mystery regarding the Charter granted to the first Prince of Wales. He blamed Henry VII for restoring the Duchy of Lancaster, and he also implied, although he did not actually say so, that he was also to be blamed for making his son, Arthur, Prince of Wales. (Before that date there had been no Prince of the whole of Wales).

(II.) The second point in Burke's speech was that it was a waste of money to maintain this provincial separation. There had of recent years been a great decrease in the revenues received by the king from his estates in Wales, and it had not been found possible to increase them. With the exception of Montgomeryshire, the king was Lord of the Manor in North Wales, and according to Professor Dodd[2], the king's rights to a great deal of common land and mountain had been forgotten, and in spite of the manorial court, free holders and tenants did not pay the rents due on much of the land. By 1787 North Wales' debts in rents to the Crown amounted to £32,000. Office-seekers and pensioners were sent to collect the debt, but Professor Dodd does not refer to John Probert, of whom Burke makes mention in his speech, the man who was sent to the mountains of North Wales to collect more money. He was paid £300 a year for his enterprise, but he failed to collect a penny.

> Probert, thus armed, and accoutred,—and paid, proceeded on his adventure;—but he was no sooner arrived on the confines of Wales, than all Wales was in arms to meet him. That nation is brave, and full of spirit. Since the invasion of King Edward, and the massacre of the bards, there never was such a tumult, and alarm, and uproar, through the region of Prestatyn. Snowdon shook to its base; Cader Edris (sic) was loosened from its foundations. The fury of litigious war blew her horn on the mountains. The rocks poured down their goatherds, and the deep caverns vomited out their miners. Every thing above ground, and every thing under ground, was in arms.
>
> In short, Sir, to alight from my Welsh Pegasus, and to come to level ground; the *preux* Chevalier Probert went to look for revenue like his masters upon other occasions; and like his masters, he found rebellion.

Although the population of Wales was but the tenth part of that of England, and her wealth only the hundredth part, yet, says Burke, there were eight judges in Wales, and but twelve in the whole of England. The provinces should therefore, be abolished by all

---

2. *The Industrial Revolution in North Wales*, A. H. Dodd, pp. 56—8.

means. The maintaining of the differences between them and England served no purpose to the king, the aristocracy, nor the people. " I propose, therefore " said Burke, " to unite all the five principalities to the Crown, and to its ordinary jurisdiction."

But he spoke differently in the House on the 20th June, 1782, and admitted that the scheme which he had proposed had failed completely.

The reform which he once intended to have made in the principality of Wales, he found was extremely unpopular in Wales ; for care had been taken to poison the minds of the Welsh, and to fill them with an idea, that the intended reform was in reality meant as an attack upon the principality ; the Welsh were full of this idea ; and so long as they were prepossessed with it, he would not force his reform upon them against their will ; he would wait till time and better information should have wrought a change in their opinion.[3]

Rhys & Jones, and Llewelyn Williams, were not correct in stating that Edmund Burke's aim was to reform the Great Sessions. His purpose was to abolish, not only the Great Sessions, but also the Principality in Wales. In spite of all his eloquent attacks on the French Revolution in his famous speeches, he advocated the same policy as that of the Jacobins, and of Napoleon after them, namely the uniting of the French provinces with the central government in Paris. In the same way as the Jacobins bound Britanny to the central authority, Burke would bind Wales closer to the central state authority in London. But it was the opposition in Wales at the end of the eighteenth century that defeated John Probert and Edmund Burke.

Burke's work was, however, continued by such Whigs as Henry Brougham, Jeremy Bentham and others. Liberty was one of the main principles of the Revolution in France. Liberty was a natural right inherent in the nature of man. The intention of the Revolution was to build a new society on this principle. The influence of the Revolution was to be seen on the English Whigs, but the liberty which they sought was of a more practical kind. It meant freedom for the individual, freedom of trade and commerce, freedom for the capitalist system, which was beginning to take shape during the latter half of the eighteenth century. Freedom was good for man, that is, for certain individuals, and was not a natural right inherent in the nature of all men as in France. Their great word was ' utility'. The good of society was the sum-total of the interests of its members. In order to facilitate the development of the individualist, capitalist system, useless time-worn institutions had to

---

3. *The Speeches*.....Vol. II, p. 357.

be abolished, and old laws and practices, based only on habit and custom, had to be done away with. The Great Sessions in Wales was one of these institutions.

In 1817, the House of Commons appointed a special committee to examine the judicial system in Wales and Cheshire. On account of the death of the Chairman, the Right Honourable George Ponsonby, it sat the second time, under the chairmanship of Earl Cawdor, and in 1821 it produced its final report. In 1828, Earl Cawdor sent a letter to Lord Lyndhurst, the Lord Chancellor, advocating the abolition of the Great Sessions, and tsating that the plan which he favoured was the one proposed by Burke half a century previously, which was to unite the province of Wales and the province of Chester to the Crown, and to bring them directly under its judicature. The intention of his plan was to unite Wales more closely with England, and to include the Welsh counties with English counties in English circuits.[4] Henry Brougham spoke in Parliament, in February 1828, on reforming the law courts and the legal system, and as a result, the Government appointed a Commission under the Lord Chancellor, to examine and to reform the common law. The law courts in Cheshire and Wales are dealt with in the first report of this Commission.[5] The Government accepted the main recommendations of the Commission, and hastened to incorporate the findings of the first report regarding law courts in Cheshire and Wales in a Parliamentary Bill. Wales, however, expressed her opinion on the matter before the Bill could be brought before Parliament.

Accounts of the meetings held in Wales are found in *Seren Gomer*, *The Cambrian Quarterly Magazine*, *The Cambrian*, and the *North Wales Chronicle*, and probably in other periodicals and newspapers which I have not been able to examine. A meeting was held in Llangefni, Anglesey, against abolishing the *Great Sessions*, although it was in favour of reform.[6] Meetings were held in Caernarvonshire, and at Ruthin in Denbighshire, and in spite of the Wynne influence[7] they were against abolition. Sir Watkin

---

4. "My hope of amendment, I confess, is in the stricter union with England and in the incorporation of Wales with other English counties, which may be convenient, into English circuits." Quoted from the letter, as published in *The Cambrian Quarterly Magazine*, Vol. 1., 1829, pp. 23—4.
5. *Reports of Commission on the Practice and Proceedings of the Courts of Common Law.* . . . .1829—1834. The title of the first report is *Despatch of Business in the Courts of Common Law at Westminster, in the Counties Palatine and in Wales—Process Serviceable or Bailable, including Original Writs, Outlawing, Arrest and Bail.*
6. *The Cambrian Quarterly Magazine*, Vol. 1, 1829, p. 119.
7. *The Cambrian Quarterly Magazine.*—Vol 1, p. 504, and the *North Wales Chronicle*, September, 24, 1829. I thank Mr. A. O. H. Jarman for the references to the latter publication.

Williams Wynne, the member for Denbighshire and Mr. Charles Watkin Williams Wynne, the member for Montgomeryshire had been against abolition in 1817, but had changed the opinion after reading Earl Cawdor's letter. I know of no report of a meeting in Merioneth, but in Radnorshire the magistrates and the free-holders declared against abolishing the Courts of Great Sessions. According to the account,[8] Aberaeron, Cardiganshire, saw the biggest meeting ever held in the county, and although Mr. Lewis Lloyd, of Dôl-haidd, and Colonel Gwynne, of Mynachty, brought forward an amendment, the original motion against abolition was carried unanimously. Two meetings were held in Carmarthenshire; the former of which, a meeting of sheriffs, justices and free-holders was held in the town of Carmarthen. It was an important meeting, for it was attended by Earl Cawdor, who was the arch-enemy of the Courts of Great Sessions, and also by Mr. John Jones, member of Parliament for Carmarthen town[9] who was the leading protagonist for the Courts. Mr. John Jones in the course of his address to this meeting claimed that there were but few in Wales in favour of abolition, and that the vast majority in Carmarthenshire, Denbighshire, Merioneth and Cardiganshire were in favour of retention. " The Welsh judicature," he said " is a gift made by Henry VIII to our forefathers and we should do all in our power to retain it." In this meeting only seventeen voted with Earl Cawdor, and the great majority with Mr. John Jones. The second meeting was held by the Borough of Carmarthen, and the motion against abolishing the Great Sessions was passed "with a large majority."[10] The Carmarthen bench of justices in the Quarter Sessions also passed a motion against abolition. In a meeting in Pembrokeshire, seven only were in favour of abolition, and the meeting held at Haverfordwest was unanimously for retention. The Glamorgan bench of magistrates was the only one to petition the Commissioners in favour of abolishing the Great Sessions, but I have not been able to trace any report of a meeting held by the people of that county.

The petitions reached the House of Commons [11] on March 9, 1830. Mr. Rice Trevor, the member for Carmarthenshire, presented the petition of Carmarthenshire freeholders against abolishing the Courts of Great Sessions; Sir J. Owen, the member for Pembrokeshire, presented the names of from 1,800 to 1,900 freeholders from his county; Mr. John Jones presented that of the Sheriffs, justices and corporation of Carmarthen, also that of the burgesses and people of Carmarthen, and another from Kidwelly; Colonel Powell, member for Cardiganshire, brought in the petition of the

8. *The Cambrian.* Nov. 21, 1829; *North Wales Chronicle,* Nov. 26, 1829.
9. *The Cambrian,* October 31, 1829; *North Wales Chronicle,* November 5th, 1829.
10. *The Cambrian,* December 30, 1829.
11. *Hansard's Parliamentary Debates,* Second series, Vol. xxiii.

freeholders of that county. Three petitions were sent to the House of Lords. Lord Dynevor presented one from the freeholders and other inhabitants of Carmarthenshire against the change contemplated in the Welsh judicature.[12] Lord Eldon presented one from the gentlemen, clergy and free-holders of Pembrokeshire against any change in the system of the Welsh judicature, and a similar petition from the mayor, burgesses and inhabitants of the town of Haverfordwest.[13] Lord Eldon pleaded in the House of Lords against the abolition of the Great Sessions. These petitions, to quote the technical language of the House, were ' left on the table', and it is on the table that they have remained.

The first reading of the bill took place in the House of Commons on March 9, 1830; the second reading on April 27, and the third on July 7 (not July 17 as wrongly stated by Rhys & Jones, and by Llewelyn Williams, for the House did not sit that day.) The amendments of the House of Lords were accepted on July 22, and the Act is dated July 23, 1830.[14] Time does not allow me to dwell on all the points raised in the various debates on the measure, and attention must be focussed on a few of them. The speech of the Attorney General, Sir J. Scarlett, during the first reading, is too legally technical for me, but I can understand the last phrase in the following sentence from his speech during the second reading—a phrase which betrays the true purpose of the bill :—

> The Welsh Courts, he said were cumbrous and expensive machines; they held ten sittings in each assize town—they hurried through cases with unseemly rapidity, allowing no chance either for compromise or accommodation; and, above all, they were different from the English Courts.[15]

He admitted that there was opposition in Wales to the measure :

> He then noticed the extreme horror which some Welsh counties seemed to entertain of being combined with others.[16]

But he did not mention the petitions against abolition which had come from Wales. He preferred to repeat the old subterfuge practised by the lawyers who framed the Act of Union, namely that the Welsh would receive the same advantages as their neighbours. The English have a genius for disguising their self-interest as magnanimity. The second reading was held at eleven o'clock at night, April 27, 1830, and Mr. John Jones, the member for Carmarthen, hinted that the Government had chosen that late hour as so many Welsh members had left, and he vainly tried to have the debate postponed.

---

12. *Ibid.*, Vol. xxii, Col. 924.
13. *Ibid.*, Vol xxiii, March 25, 1830.
14. An Act for the more effectual administration of Justice in England and Wales. *The Statutes*..... Vol. iv.
15. Hansard.....Vol. xxiii, Col. 1179.
16. *Ibid.*, Vol. xxiii, Col 1180.

In his speech in the second debate he said that the members of the
Common Law Commission—Sergeant Bosanquet, H. J. Stephen,
E. Hall Alaerson, James Parker, and John Patteson—were unacquainted with Wales, and that they had never been in a Welsh court.
He noted on their Report that they had received a petition from 23
persons in Cardiganshire in favour of abolishing the Court of Great
Sessions, but there were more than that number of respected persons
in Cardiganshire, and the twenty-three did not include the Powells,
the Prices, and the Lloyds, not to mention Colonel Powell, the
member for the county. On the petition sent to them from Carmarthenshire, by an agent of Lord Cawdor, and bearing the names
of only four or five people, it was suggested that thousands more
signatures could have been obtained had time permitted, but the
Earl was only able to secure seventeen votes at the meeting held in
Carmarthen. Two counties only, in the whole of Wales, had declared for abolition and in one of them, the declaration had been
made by a small group of persons, namely the magisterial bench.
Moreover, the English themselves had agreed that certain features
of the Welsh judicial system were better than the corresponding
features in the English system. Legal records from Welsh counties
were also borne to the Chancery in London, and these records
were the bases of legal property in Wales. Mr. John Jones agreed,
as others did in periodicals[17] and newspapers, that it was the poor
who would feel the loss of the Great Sessions, for litigation was
cheaper in Wales than in England, and verdicts more expeditiously
given, whereas if the Courts of Great Sessions were abolished, the
poor would not be able to take their cases to London, and bear the
costs, not only of lawyers and witnesses, but also of translators.
The rich alone would be able to meet these costs, and that was why
some of them were for abolition.

Mr. Rice Trevor agreed that the real purpose of abolishing the
Great Sessions was in order to obtain three more judges to the
twelve already at Westminster Hall, but why should Wales have to
sacrifice her separate judicature for that purpose ? Abolition would
mean greater costs and inconvenience to Wales, indeed, the cost of
the correspondence between Wales and Westminster Hall was likely
to be greater than the whole cost of conducting the case in a Welsh
court. Sir John Owen held that he was in favour of reforming legal
administration in Wales, but that the majority of the Welsh people
were opposed to abolition of the Great Sessions, as they looked on
these Courts as one of their greatest privileges. Mr. Charles Watkin
Wynne, member for Montgomeryshire, was in favour of abolition,
and the following was his main argument : —

---

17. An excellent article, for example, in *The Cambrian Quarterly Magazine*, Vol. 1, 1829, pp. 249—259.

The principle was, to complete the union between England and Wales and give Wales the benefit of English judicature.[18]

Colonel Wood, the member for Brecknockshire, was also for abolition, but he was against uniting Welsh with English counties in the same circuits, and he maintained that jurymen should be Welsh-speaking Welshmen, for the use of English in law courts in Wales was as odious as would be the use of French in the law courts of England. Sir Christopher Cole, the member for Glamorgan, was also for abolition and Mr. Frankland Lewis, the member for Radnorshire, sat on the fence.

We thus see that the Welsh people, taking them all in all, were fairly unanimous against the abolition of the Courts of Great Sessions, but that their representatives in Parliament, particularly the Wynnes, and other titled members, were not so unanimous. It is true that it was on account of distance from London, and not as a recognition in any way by the Tudor lawyers of Welsh national unity that Wales had been granted this Court in the reign of Henry VIII (Monmouthshire did not come within its authority on the grounds of its greater proximity to London), but it is equally clear that by the end of the eighteenth century, and the beginning of the nineteenth century, the Welsh had grown to regard the Court of Great Sessions as a national institution. Edmund Burke heeded her voice in 1782, but the English Whigs paid no regard to Welsh opinion in 1830. By the beginning of the nineteenth century, Britain was united. Wales had been joined to England in 1536 —1542, Scotland in 1707, and Ireland in 1801 ; thus by the begining of the century all political power had been centralised in the London Parliament, and the English in that assembly could outvote the combined representatives of the three other nations. The next step of Government policy was to eliminate all remaining independence in the three subject countries. Historians tell us that in the abolition of the Great Sessions was eliminated the last institution granted to Wales by the Tudors, but one institution still remained and that was the Principality. It is the Principality, together with the Welsh language, which have kept Wales from becoming an English county like Cornwall.

One need only touch lightly on the influence of the French Revolution on a few Welsh men of letters, as books and chapters have already appeared on the subject. John Jones of Glan-y-gors, Thomas Roberts of Llwynrhudol, Morgan John Rhys, Tomos Glyn Cothi, and others, loudly praised the rights of man; they attacked the monarchy, the episcopate and the aristocracy (although Glan-y-gors commended the generosity of the old squires of the past,

---

18. *Hansard.* Second series, vol. xxiii, col. 114.

whilst holding that that generosity had itself been buried in the grave of Sir Watkin Williams Wynne); they called for the abolition of tithes and taxes, and for a general secret ballot on the pattern of that of the Gwyneddigion Society. The best feature of the Revolution in France was the transfer of much of the land from the hands of the king, the Church, and the aristocracy, to those of the peasantry, but these Welsh writers did not urge a similar reform in England and Wales, and neither did they follow Ellis Wynne's attacks in *Y Bardd Cwsg* on land enclosures. In their books and magazines they discussed all kinds of freedom except a nation's freedom. Although they were true Welshmen, and worthy of all praise for writing in Welsh, and for pleading the cause of the language, there was nothing nationally Welsh in their politics. That was British. The French Revolution stimulated national movements in some European counties, and its national influence can be seen in Ireland in the politics of Wolfe Tone, and of Daniel O'Connell, but the Welsh writers we have in mind spoke only of abolishing the English monarchy, and of reforming the British Parliament. The outlook of Glan-y-gors, Llwynhudol, and the others, became that of our nineteenth century Radicals and Liberals, minus their Republicanism. The reforms suggested by Glan-y-gors and his group were postponed as a result of the war between France and Britain.

The French War was the severest fought by Britain up to that time, and bore considerable resemblance to that of 1939—45. Napoleon, like Hitler, strove to make Europe an economic unit directed against Britain. The French threatened to land on her shores, and some of them succeeded to do so at Fishguard; a 'homeguard' watched the beaches, the French also threatened to land in Ireland; Prussia and Russia partitioned Poland; Britain was nearly starved; there was a great stimulus to agriculture, and also to industry for munition purposes. After the war, there was a conflict between the claims of agriculture and industry, but that is another story.

The many changes in the first half of the nineteenth century were not accomplished without opposition, conflict and rioting. There was revolt in town and country. In 1811 and 1812 the Luddites tried to smash machinery; the Peterloo slaughter occurred in 1819; the chartists attacked London, Birmingham and Bristol, and in the Swing Movement, England saw something similar to our Rebecca risings. There were a number of strikes in Wales, particularly the Merthyr strike of 1831, the Rebecca movement arose in five counties of South Wales and the Chartists arose in Llanidloes and Newport. It was John Frost, Dic Penderyn, Dai'r Cantwr, a⁻ d Shoni Sgubor-fawr, who drew the attention of the English

Government to Wales, and incurred its wrath. The Government simply had to put an end to rebellion in England and Wales, particularly in Wales, for should not the barbarians of that country be thankful and content after the abolition of the Great Sessions and the extension to them of the blessings of English law ? A means had to be found of subjecting them, and that means was education, state education.

In the House of Commons, on the 10th of March, 1846, Mr. William Williams, the member for Coventry, requested the Government to send a Crown Commission to examine the state of education in Wales, and to discover what facilities existed there to teach English to the people. I shall mention a few points in Mr. Williams's speech.[19] He stated that enquiries had been made into the state of education in every part of England, Scotland and Ireland, but not in Wales, and that a splendid system of education had been set up in Ireland, a system which would remove all the ills of that distracted country, and lead her to a state of Irish prosperity. Nationalists like Thomas Davis, were not of the same opinion as Mr. Williams regarding this system of education. It was a noble tribute to that system that Irishmen were dying of hunger owing to the failure of the potato crop, and to the fact that wheat was being filched from the country, at the very time that Mr. Williams was addressing Parliament. He also held that Scotland, too, had had an excellent system of education, for it had succeeded in eliminating every difference between a Scot and an Englishman.

> If the Welsh had the same advantage for education as the Scotch, they would, instead of appearing a distinct people in no respect differ from the English. Would it not, then, be wisdom and sound policy to send the English schoolmaster among them ? [20]

He stated that the greatest obstacle in Wales was the Welsh language :—

> The people of that country laboured under a peculiar difficulty from the existence of an ancient language.[21]

Government Commissions of the past had conclusively proved that point. Mr. Tremenheere [22] had conducted an enquiry into the Welsh parts around Newport, where there had been Chartist risings, and at Merthyr Tydfil, and had shown in his Report that

---

19. The complete speech can be read in *Hansard*, vol. lxxxiv, Tuesday, March 10, 1846.
20. *Hansard*, Vol. lxxxiv, Col 853.
21. *Ibid.* Col. 846.
22. *Minutes of the Committee of Council on Education.* . . .1839—40. Appendix II. Report of Mr. Seymour Tremenheere on the State of Elementary Education in the Mining District of South Wales.

in 18 only of 47 schools in these parts was English taught, and that of the few who were literate among the ninety who attended evening classes, a goodly proportion were monoglot Welsh. Mr. Williams also referred to the report of the Rev. H. L. Ballairs, who had carried out an enquiry in the same districts on behalf of a committee of the Education Council of the Privy Council.

It should be borne in mind that an ill-educated and undisciplined population, like that existing amongst the mines in South Wales, is one that may be found most dangerous to the neighbourhood in which it dwells and that a band of efficient schoolmasters is kept up at a much less expense than a body of police or soldiery.

A schoolmaster was better than a policeman, and schools were cheaper than soldiers. The purpose of education was to make the Welsh, particularly the industrial workers of South Wales, obedient, respectful, and serviceable in the new capitalist system. Mr. Williams, in his speech, blamed the capitalists in Wales for not having raised schools to teach the workers to save money, and censured the landlords for not realising that they stood to gain tenfold from their lands, if their tenants were only instructed and made to understand. He also stated that he was of the same opinion as the Commission which had sat to enquire into the causes of the Rebecca riots, and had found that ignorance of English was one of these causes. He quoted from this Report [23]:—

It would be improper to pass unnoticed amongst the causes which affect the social condition of the people, the ignorance of the English language which pervades so large a portion of the country,.. .. ..

The Government was also at fault for since 1839, it had spent £248,000 on education in Great Britain, and the five counties of South Wales affected by the Rebecca risings had received only £2,176; Staffordshire with a population of 500,000, like the whole of South Wales, had received £14,575 for education, which was seven times as much. *The Times* also sent a correspondent to Carmarthenshire to enquire into the causes of these risings, and he also found that ignorance of English in those parts was one of the causes.[24] Mr. Williams also dealt with the use of the Welsh language in law courts in Wales, giving examples to show how it hindered the course of justice, and he quoted from the Report of the Queen's Commission on the administration of justice in Wales.

---

23. Report of the Commissioners of Inquiry for South Wales. 1844.
24. *Hansard.* Vol. LXXXIV. Col. 850.

The people's ignorance of the English language, practically prevents the working of the laws and institutions, and impedes the administration of justice.[25]

Sir James Graham replied for the Government, and agreed with Mr. Williams that knowledge of English would be of great benefit to the people of Wales. As Mr. Williams had stated, the system of education in Scotland was excellent, and it was the intention of the Government, under God's blessing, to grant a similar system to Wales. He said, furthermore, that the Government could not appoint a Commission under the Crown, but that the Committee of the Privy Council would appoint Inspectors to carry out the examination, upon which Mr. Williams withdrew his motion, and accepted the Government proposal.

The last to speak was Mr. Williams Wynne, who said that he knew little of South Wales, but that he did know North Wales, and that he could tesify that the landlords of the North had not forgotten their duties to the peasantry, and that both Churchmen and Nonconformists had been busy setting up schools in every parish The difficulty in the North was the large extent of some of the parishes, and the difficulty in the South was the sudden rise in population; hence a system of education could not be set up in the twinkling of an eye.

Towards the end of 1847, the Inspectors, Mr. Lingen, Mr. H R. Vaughan Johnson, and Mr. Jelinger Cookson Symonds published their Reports separately. The following year, Mr. William Williams published two letters, *A Letter to the Right Honourable Lord John Russell* and *A Second Letter on the present defective state of education in Wales*. The purpose of the two letters was to induce the Government to convert the recommendations of " The Blue Books " into a Parliamentary Bill. The accusations against Wales in these books were countered by Ieuan Gwynedd, Henry Richard, Gwilym Hiraethog, Thomas Phillips, Dr. Lewis Edwards, the Dean of Bangor, R. J. Derfel, Miss Jane of Williams Ysgafell, Owen Owen Roberts, and others.

I am only concerned in this address with the attitude taken towards Wales in 'The Blue Books,' and towards her literature, and the Welsh language, and I shall endeavour to be brief. According to these Books, it was one of the disadvantages of Welsh that it was only the language of agriculture and theology. The language isolated Wales from the world (that is, from England and the British Empire); it kept the Welsh from succeeding in business and commerce; it hindered the middle class in Wales from advancement

---

25. *Ibid.* Col. 860.

and success. Welsh was also an obstacle in law courts because the monoglot Welsh had an advantage over the magistrates and judges ! It should be noted that it was not the Welsh, but the English who were handicapped in the Courts. Some of the ' monoglot ' Welsh had a smattering of English, and when the Judge asked a question in English, *via* the interpreter, the wily Welshman understood him, and had time to think of an answer while the translating was taking place. He could not, therefore, be confused by rapid questioning, and caught out by a hasty reply. The Welsh language slowed down the whole legal process. Ieuan Gwynedd's reply was that the laws should be translated to Welsh, instead of retaining the use of English for the convenience of a few judges.

It was also held against the Welsh language that it had no literature of any value. Mr. Williams argued that it had no ' useful literature', and he was quite right, for it did not tell how to make money nor how to exploit Welsh resources to the advantage of the English. Mr. Johnson, one of the Inspectors, appended to his Report a list of 405 books in Welsh, but Ieuan Gwynedd said that he could add another two hundred, and we know today of many more. Ieuan Gwynedd rightly held that the purpose of Mr. William Williams, and of the " Blue Books " was to foist a state system of education on Wales, to enforce the use of English, and to kill the Welsh language. The truth of his allegations has been borne out by the Education Act of 1870.

According to some of the witnesses as recounted in ' The Blue Books', ignorance of English was one reason for the Rebecca and Chartist risings, and we have already seen that this was one of Mr. Tremenheere's conclusions in his Report, as also of the *Times*' correspondent, and of Mr. Williams in his speech in Parliament. On this point ' The Blue Books ' are like a court with its verdict already decided before it has sat. Ieuan Gwynedd and Henry Richard replied that it was the English who were to blame for the Chartist attack on Newport. Ieuan Gwynedd also held that the landlords were to blame for the Rebecca risings, and not the peasantry, and that the Swing Movement was a similar outbreak in England. Basically, the Rebecca risings were a revolt against the capitalist system in agriculture, and the Chartists were in revolt against industrial capitalism, although capitalists reaped the advantages of their labour and sacrifice. Ieuan Gwynedd and Henry Richard give the impression that they did not approve of the restlessness and revolt in Wales, and the main weakness of their arguments is that they maintain that the Welsh were the most religious, moral, and cultured nation under the sun, and that they formed the most loyal and peace-loving nation in the British Empire. Their opponents took advantage of this weakness.

By studying the Reports of Government Commissions, from that of the Commission on the Common Law to ' The Blue Books', it can be seen that the definite and constant aim of the English Government was to kill the Welsh language, and to enforce English. The Government saw, and that quite correctly, that Wales could not be completely united to England without destroying the language for this was the main partition wall. She was the leper who shook her bell to keep the English away. After the elimination of the Great Sessions, the Welsh language was the sand in the legal machinery of Westminster Hall ; she was the greatest obstruction to the English capitalist system, the sprag in the wheel of the Act of Union. The language had been kept alive by the Welsh translation of the Bible, by the books and periodicals published by Churchmen and Nonconformists, by the circulating schools of Griffith Jones of Llanddowror, and the Sunday Schools of Thomas Charles of Bala, but it had not been foreseen that the language would be such a political force in the middle of the nineteenth century. The most important thing was not the language in itself, but the things taught through the language : religion, history, theology and literature. The enforcement of English has not been the greatest evil, but through the English language to enforce secularism on Wales. In these last days we have seen the bountiful blessings which have come to men in the wake of secularism, and not only to men, but also to rats, goats and swine.

(II). 1850—1880.

The main event within this period, and indeed the most important event in the whole history of Welsh national movements throughout the century, was the emigration to Patagonia. This emigration cannot be understood apart from its historical background.

The period from about 1850 to the years around 1880 is known as the Victorian Golden Age. Before 1847, gold was scarce in the Bank of England, so scarce that some believed that silver would have to replace it as a standard of currency, but gold was discovered that year in California, and later in Australia, and there was an unexampled revival in business and commerce. The International Exhibition of 1851, in the Crystal Palace, was a symbol of this revival— the exhibition described by Talhaiarn in prose and song as the 'World's Fair'. The Reform Acts of 1832 and 1868 placed the Government in the hands of the capitalists, and Free Trade brought economic power to their tentacles. Cobden and Bright, together with their Welsh disciples, Gwilym Hiraethog, S. R. and Henry Richard, imagined that Free Trade would draw nations nearer to each other, and abolish war, but they did not see that material interest and imperial pride can lurk behind trade, whether it be free or controlled. It was a period of bright success in the worlds of capital and labour, a period of sunshine between two storms, a treacherous sunshine. Wages were comparatively high, sufficiently high for money to be saved, and placed in banks for investment in industry. Men of religion, educationalists and statemen taught the value of saving economy, providence, temperance, and hard work. *Laissez faire* pleased capitalists and workers, for was it not one of the laws of the Almighty?

Between 1841 and 1852 the railways came to Wales with their threat to the last ramparts of the Welsh language and the culture of our countryside, both of which had up to that time been comparatively safe in the country districts; and also in many of the industrial areas, in view of the fact that the country immigrants to these areas brought with them their habits of speech, their culture, and their religion. The danger arose, not from the railways themselves, for these could be made useful tools to rebuild Wales and be of spiritual benefit. The harm came from the materialism and the cult of Mammon which they transported into the country. They were English railways, meant to link South Wales with London, Mid-Wales with Shrewsbury, and the North with Liverpool. Talhaiarn, Ceiriog, Iago Emlyn and others living around the mid-century believed that the railways spelt the doom of the Welsh language and folk-culture. A cartoon in the Welsh *Punch* showed a woman in Welsh costume vainly trying to stop a steam-engine on a railway with her umbrella. A correspondent writing in *Y Celt* on the 17th March, 1893, said that "about thirty years ago, or perhaps a little more, following the penetration of the railway to the country districts, there came an English wave to throw its spume throughout Wales to the horror of many who believed that that wave was going to drown Welsh Wales in a trice."

Time does not allow me to dwell on the attacks of certain English periodicals and books on Wales. At the beginning of the century, the *Sun* attacked the petitions against the abolition of the Courts of Great Sessions, and at a later date such papers as *The Morning Chronicle* and *The Examiner* attacked the Welsh language, the Eisteddfod, the Gorsedd, and other national traits. I give only two quotations, taken from one book, namely *Lady Cambria*, by H. L. Spring, 1867. Here is Mr. Spring's opinion:—

> Had the mineral wealth of the principality been discovered by the natives, and could it have been properly put to use before they were subdued to English rule, they might have preserved their language and have been the foremost

amongst British subjects in wealth, manufactures and arts; but as the English have, through Providence, been the means of opening out her resources, it is plain that the English element must universally prevail. (p. 49).

The trouble about the Welsh, as has also been said by others before, and after him, was that they did not respect their conquerors:

> .... the Welsh are a conquered race, and have very little regard for their conquerors, and even some of the most ignorant of them are so stupid as to entertain the notion of reclaiming their country from the English, and fancy that it would not be a difficult thing to take possession of the railways in the principality.

That is a confession on behalf of his nation by an honest Englishman that Wales was under an English capitalist system. The purpose of this system was to reap the last fruits of the death of Llywelyn our last prince, the conquest of Owain Glyndŵr, and the Union of Wales with England.

The greatest danger arose not from English attacks on Wales, but from Welsh weakness. R. J. Derfel, Michael D. Jones, and Emrys ap Iwan strove against these weaknesses. From their writings we may gather that the burden of the attacks of the anglicised Welsh against the language was that it was merely the speech of agriculture, and poverty; that her literature was of meagre value, that no Shakespeare or Milton had arisen in Wales; that English was the language of trade and commerce, of affluence and success, and that before long it would be the language of the world. For the sake of these anglicised Welsh, clergy would turn their services to English, Nonconformists would build English chapels, and when some preachers were forbidden to preach in English, they would set about erecting seceding English chapels, and would introduce English to the Sunday Schools. As you are acquainted with the works of R. J. Derfel and Emrys ap Iwan, I shall quote a passage or two from those of Michael D. Jones:

> The cry in our midst for English chapels in which Welsh people may worship is a step in that direction. I hold that the greater part of the demand among us for English chapels arises from the haughty pride of men made servile by adulation of the English. . . . . .We have many families who are doing their best to bring up their children English-speaking, and in ignorance of Welsh. To the best of their ability they are planting anti-Welsh feelings and principles in the rising generation. . . Why do so many of our ministers of religion support this attitude ? [26]

---

26. *Y Ddraig Goch.* June 1877, pp. 65, 6.

Michael D. Jones saw that Welsh people in Wales and in the United States, in losing their language lost also their culture, their ways of life, and their religion:

Moreover, is it not worth while maintaining our language our customs, our religion, and ways of life as a nation ? And does not our history as a nation, on both sides of the Atlantic prove that in losing our language, we almost invariably lose as well the other qualities mentioned, at least to a certain extent, and often completely ? And what do we get in exchange from the English for our language, customs, religion and way of life ? Do we get knowledge and civilisation ? [27]

In spite of all the attacks which have been made against the " Treason of the Blue Books", it should be remembered that the point of view expressed in these " Books " was that of these Anglophile Welsh; this middle class—tradesmen, capitalists and professional men—and also their imitators among the common people. They were the disciples of Mr. William Williams, the member for Coventry. The impression one gets in reading the history of this period is that the religious revivals of the first half of the century had been extinguished with Californian gold.

In this crisis in our nation's history, and it was one of the major crises, God raised great leaders for Wales : Gwilym Hiraethog, S.R., Henry Richard, Ieuan Gwynedd, Thomas Gee, R. J. Derfel, Michael D. Jones, and others, but the greatest of these were the three nationalists, Thomas Gee, R. J. Derfel, and Michael D. Jones. I need only name Thomas Gee, as Dr. T. Gwynn Jones has written an excellent biography of him ; I have elsewhere discussed the place of R. J. Derfel in the history of nineteenth century Welsh nationalism. Michael D. Jones's biography has been written by E. Pan Jones, but although the author has very assiduously collected many facts, he was too near to him, and himself too much a product of the same period, to be able to see Michael D. Jones in his entirety. Michael D. Jones was a saint ; a great and largehearted Congregationalist ; the greatest Welshman of the nineteenth century ; our greatest nationalist after Owain Glyndŵr. Three things at least made him a nationalist :—

(1) *The influence of Louis Kossuth.*—I have elsewhere dealt with the influence of the great Hungarian leader on R. J. Derfel and others, but his influence on Michael D. Jones was even greater. He paid a tribute to him in his article on " Self-Government " in *Y Celt*, March 7., 1890—

Kossuth, the world-famous Hungarian patriot like a bright star in the firmament of Europe, had fired many a soul with the immortal doctrine of the ' right of every nation to

---

27. *Oes a Gwaith. . . .Michael D. Jones. . . .*p. 42.

self-government', and between the influence of the great revolutions of 1848, and the teachings of Kossuth, the conquered nations of Europe are no longer appeased, but look forward hopefully towards the jubilee of oppressed[28] nations and peoples.

If the French Revolution failed to have a *nationalist effect* on Wales, the émigrés of the national movements which arose in various European countries following the Napoleonic wars, such as Garibaldi, Mazzini, and Kossuth, did have such an influence.

(II.) *His wide knowledge of Welsh and English History.*—After we have read the articles of R. J. Derfel and Michael D. Jones, we find nothing new in those of Emrys ap Iwan except their style, and Michael D. Jones based his arguments on Welsh history to a greater extent than Emrys ap Iwan. Jac Glan-y-gors saw English history from the age of Hengist and Horsa to his own day as a record of corrupt monarchies; Michael D. Jones saw the same long period as a record of English oppression of Wales. Both were radicals but the former was a Welsh radical, and the latter a Welsh national one.

(III.) *Seeing Welsh people becoming imitation Englishmen in Wales, and imitation Yankees in North America.*—It is surprising that this man, who was our greatest nationalist became the father of an emigration from Wales. Let us try to understand the reasons for this.

(i) Emigration was taking place, and could not be hindered. Michael D. Jones had been a minister of a church in Cincinnati, Ohio, and had seen there, and in other States, that there was no independence for the Welsh. They had no choice but to be absorbed by the Yankees. And moreover, rich Welsh North Americans invited poor people from Wales to come to them as hewers of wood and drawers of water. At first he believed that Wisconsin was the State most suitable for Welsh emigration, as that State had translated its Constitution into Welsh for the sake of its Welsh settlers, but he later changed his opinion. He saw that the only policy was to use the emigration movement for his own purpose.

(ii.) He saw that Wales could not be freed in his own day, because of English domination and Welsh servility, English landlordism in rural districts, and English capitalism in the industrial parts. Wales could only solve the Land Question, and the problem of

---

28. *Oes a Gwaith y Prif Athraw y Parch. Michael Daniel Jones* gan E. Pan Jones, Ph.D., M.A., Mostyn, 1903.

Capital and Labour in another country. The founding of the Welsh colony in Patagonia can only be understood against this background.

(a) *The Land Question.*—This was one of the most important issues during the last century, but I have time only to touch on it lightly. The usual belief is that the Welsh colonists fled from the tithes, and the taxes, from domination and oppression; and that is true, but there was a reason that went deeper, namely the ownership of land. The instinct for ownership is healthy, but like every other instinct it must be kept under control. The unjust thing is to have too much property in the hands of too few, and for the State to own everything is worse than landlordism. The instinct for property was stifled among Welsh people by landlordism, and from this repression arose the dream of ownership of land in ' The New Country '. The ' Farmer's Paradise ' in Patagonia is described in an article in *Y Ddraig Goch.*

> In the Welsh Colony, on the banks of the Camwy, everyone lives on his own land. The farmer need not share the fruits of his labour with anyone, but with his family. A 236 acre farm on the banks of the Camwy is given to each family that chooses to go there—given for nothing, and for ever.[19]

Michael D. Jones saw that the Welsh, through the ownership of land, could become a free and responsible people. The Welsh could rule in Patagonia, and not only serve as in Wales.

> Our national weakness at present is our servility, but in a Welsh Colony we can be imbued with a new spirit.[30]

And again :—

> The intention of the friends of the Welsh Colony is to find a place where the Welsh people can be a formative element. [31]

Michael D. Jones, as a practical nationalist, saw that ownership of land would give dignity and independence to the Welsh people; and not only that, but also an opportunity to become a " formative element", that is, a freedom to rule, to govern themselves. There were other Welsh emigrations, but the emigration to Patagonia was a national emigration.

---

29. *Y Ddraig Goch.*—A monthly magazine to serve the Welsh Colony, edited by the Rev. R. Mawddwy Jones, Dolwyddelen. Vol. 1, No. 1, January 1876, p. 8. This Magazine was first published in 1862, but there are no issues in the National Library of Wales earlier than 1876.
30 *Oes a Gwaith. . . . Michael D. Jones*, pp. 171—2.
31. *Ibid*, p. 171.

(b) *Capital and Labour.*—Unlike all the other Liberals, Michael D. Jones, saw in Capitalism as great a curse to Wales as landlordism.

> The resources of Wales—her coal, iron, slates, lead, and brass are greater than the resources of California if we suppose that that state has only gold ![32]

But these resources were utilised and developed by the English.

> Generally speaking, Welsh resources are developed by English companies, Englishmen take the profits, and Welshmen do the work.[33]

In a pamphlet published to encourage emigration to Patagonia, re-published later in *Y Ddraig Goch*, and bearing a title which may be translated " A Few Things Workers will find worth knowing",[34] an " Old Country", and a " New Country " are contrasted with each other as follows :—

In an OLD COUNTRY :—
(1) *Land* is *scarce.*
(2) *Capital* is *scarce.*
(3) There is a *glut* of workers.

In a NEW COUNTRY :
(1) *Land* is *free.*
(2) *Less Capital* is *sufficient.*
(3) *Labour* is *scarce.*

> The valuable thing in an *old country* is what the worker *does not possess.* In a *new country* the valuable thing is what the worker *possesses.* Therefore EMIGRATION is the hope of Welsh workers.

This article also shows how to plan and set up factories and industries.

> Let us assume that a hundred workers unite to work a factory, a quarry, a coal mine, etc. :—
> (1) They must pick five or seven of the most intelligent among themselves to form a committee.
> (2) The Committee must appoint officials—a chairman, treasurer, and secretary.
> (3) They must then appoint a steward, and all other essential officers.

---

32. *Oes a Gwaith.* . . . *Michael D. Jones,* p. 168.
33. *Ibid.* p. 175.
34. *Y Ddraig Goch.* Vol II, No. 20, August 1877.

(4) The Steward must allot the work and wages of each worker. Let every worker be paid the customary rates.

(5) At the end of the year, let the profit be divided to every one in the ratio of his wages. This plan will show that the *knowledge* possessed by the workers will enable them to do without the *supervision of an employer*, hence they will receive his portion in addition to their wages. *This implies making the best use of labour.*

The above is an outline of a co-operative plan of industry. In his important article on " Co-operative Companies,"[35] Michael D. Jones stated that Mr. Dafydd Llwyd Jones, formerly of Ffestiniog, was the leading apostle of the co-operative principle in the Welsh Colony," and that the Colony's big mistake was to " lose control of the railways, and the lands of Port Madryn to English companies, when with a little co-operation they could in a short time have worked them themselves". He urged workers in Wales to pay attention to the co-operative movement.

. . . . . . .and the movement deserves much greater attention from the working class in Wales than it has received.

Lewis Jones, in his book on the history of the Welsh Colony gives much useful information about the Colony, such as that there was no difference there between North Walians and South Walians, nor any enmity between Church and Nonconformity, and no struggle between Tory, Liberal and Socialist, but the most important part of the book is the description of the co-operative social system of the Colony.

In glancing on the situation of the three thousand Welsh people here, who are living in community with each other, a group of ordinary working people from the Old Country, transplanted into a soil quite different from that in which they grew, one sees that the aspects of community life which we have evolved are exceedingly new and interesting. The grazing together of our flocks and herds, the joint-purchasing of equipment until we become strong enough, the joint-threshing, the working together to dig long canals, and the pooling of resources in buying and selling, together with the joint-control over our affairs and our joint-efforts to secure our rights as a community,—a glance at all these things show that a pattern of life quite different to anything in Wales has been formed".[36]

---
35. *Y Celt*, June 6, 1890.
36. *Hanes y Wladva Gymreig*, by L. J. Plas Hedd, p. 187.

The Land Problem, and the relationship of Capital and Labour were solved in the Welsh Colony as they should have been solved. The co-operative plan was there in operation both in agriculture and industry.

The Patagonian Colony was Michael D. Jones's Christian nationalist creation. The reading of his articles and speeches shows that his purpose was to plant a free Wales on Patagonian soil; a Wales with its own Senate, with the Red Dragon flying over its tower, and the Welsh language used officially within it; a Wales with her language taught in her schools; a Wales conducting business and commerce in her own language; a Wales maintaining her religion, her culture, and her institutions; a country with its own independent judicature, with her laws in her own language; a land where her farmers owned " their land, and her workers controlled her industry." But Michael D. Jones made one grave miscalculation; he thought that the Spaniards, unlike the North Americans, would allow to the Welsh their freedom and independence.

" Planting ten or twenty thousand Welsh people among illiterate and unskilled Spaniards, will certainly give the advantage to the Welsh, as long as they secure education, commerce, and laws in their own language. . . . .Welsh among Spaniards will not meet with the same fate, as among North Americans, who are energetic, and who draw every nation into their own mould.[37]"

We see today that centralised government in the Argentine, and Welsh inability to resist it, can put an end to Michael D. Jones's free Wales, but if that were to happen completely, it would still remain as an ideal, and more than an ideal, an inspiration and a pattern. Wales was liberated in Patagonia. It should, however, be remembered that she was liberated by an adventurous spirit, persistency, a belief in definite principles, and self-sacrifice. Some of Michael D. Jones's contemporaries laughed at his home-spun clothes, and I have heard the same laughter from some of our present-day slick historians—as if he were merely a suit of clothes. Little have they seen of the large holes which his nationalism had burnt in his broad-cloth pockets. Bodiwan, and the grave in Rhos-y-fedwen Cemetery should be places of pilgrimage not only for all nationalists, but for all true Welshman.

(III) 1880—1900.

The most important feature of this period was the *Cymru Fydd* Movement. Tom Ellis, Lloyd George, O. M. Edwards, and others who led were disciples of Michael D. Jones. The

---

37. *Oes a Gwaith. . . . Michael D. Jones*, pp. 189—190.

movement would not have been possible without his influence, but not one of his disciples equalled him as a nationalist, and not one of them matched him in strength and integrity of character.

The year 1895 was the greatest in the history of Welsh national movements in the last twenty years of the century. Early that year, four Welsh M.P.'s on account of the dilatoriness of the Government in passing Welsh measures such as the Land Reform and the Dissestablishment of the Church, formed an independent party. These four were Lloyd George, Herbert Lewis, Frank Edwards, and D. A. Thomas. Lord Rosebery, the Prime Minister, was somewhat alarmed. He promised to place Disestablishment at the head of his programme, and the independent party ceased to be. In January, 1895, the Prime Minister came to Cardiff to address the " National Liberal Federation",[38] and said that the best thing for Wales would be to secure her own Parliament, where the Disestablishment Bill could be passed, as the English people had no interest in that measure. The most important political article in *Young Wales* is that by Lloyd George on " National Self-Government for Wales".[39] The purpose of the article is to explain why the Tories defeated the Liberals in the 1895 election. He held that one reason for the severe defeat of the latter was their refusal to grant Home Rule to Ireland. The Celts in 1885 were where they were in 1868, and in the same place in 1895 as in 1885, but the Teutons were unstable and vacillating. It is a fashionable thing among the English to change their government. The Home Rule Bill formulated under Gladstone in 1886 was a hurried and insufficient measure, and it was a foolish thing to offer to the Irish a Parliament for Irish matters only, and to expect the Irish Members to come to Westminster to discuss Imperial matters: such a solution would be beyond the wit even of Mr. Gladstone, and moreover, the Irish votes could defeat the Government on an Imperial issue. (I should add that what the Liberals dreaded was that Ireland would secede from the Empire if Home-Rule were granted). In 1893, Gladstone had his second opportunity to give Home Rule to Ireland, but his Bill of that year was hardly better than that of 1886, and this time the suggestion was made that the Irish Members should be kept in Westminster, but that their number should be reduced. As a result, the Irish Members of Parliament went over to the Tories in the election of 1895, and that was one reason for the fall of the Liberals. (The Irish cared nothing for Liberalism or Toryism, but only for Ireland, and the Liberals and Tories did not care at all for Ireland, but only for the votes of her members in Westminster).

---

38. A report of the meeting and a summary of the speech can be found in *Baner ac Amserau Cymru*, January 26, 1895.

39. *Young Wales*, Vol. I, No. 10, October 1895.

The only hope of the Liberals, said Lloyd George in his article, was to grant Home Rule all round. Teutons and Celts could not hit it off together :

> It all arises from the fact that it is quite impossible to have one legislature to serve the needs of Celt and Teuton. . . . . .It is abundantly clear that no nation with self-respect can endure such a state of affairs without making a determined attempt at reform.

Let us accept then, says Lloyd-George, the offer of Lord Rosebery, made in his Cardiff speech; let us insist on a Parliament for Wales, and there let us enact the Disestablishment of the Church. But in the December issue we see that objection has been raised to Lloyd George's suggestion regarding a Welsh Parliament.

> We regret that that contribution, (*i.e.* Lloyd George's speech) has been greatly misunderstood. Lloyd George did not wish, as some of his critics have stated, to give Disestablishment a second place in our programme.

Lord Rosebery's offer of a Welsh Parliament was thus refused. The leaders of the Cymru Fydd Movement, Lloyd George, Tom Ellis, Elphin, Herbert Lewis, Arthur Price, W. J. Parry, and others, were nationalists, but the bulk of the rank and file of the movement held them back and obstructed them. The rank and file was Liberal and not Nationalist. There is much truth in the following description of the movement :—

" Cymru Fydd is Liberalism in Welsh costume."[40]

Baner ac Amserau Cymru, April 3, 1895, contains a report of a resolution passed in Parliament under the caption, " Home Rule all round. The principle confirmed." The resolution, according to the *Baner* was proposed by Mr. Dalziel, member for Birmingham, in the following words :—

> That this House is of the opinion, that in order to give more direct and fuller effect to the wishes and special needs of the different nations which compose the United Kingdom, and in order to add to the effectiveness of the Imperial Parliament, it would be expedient to transfer to separate legislatures in Ireland, Scotland, Wales and England, the control and government of their respective home affairs.

The proposal was seconded by Mr. Lloyd George, who held that what Wales required was a Parliament for home affairs, and that she did not desire to have her own army or navy. " He stated

---

40. *Young Wales*, Vol. 5, No. 50, p. 41.

that he believed in the principle of home rule for each part of the kingdom, because by that means local patriotism could be turned to some advantage." One hundred and twenty-eight voted for the resolution, and one hundred and two against it. The Great Sessions had long been abolished, but now a Parliamentary majority voted not only for a separate judicature for Wales, but for some sort of home-rule, yet nothing further was done beyond " confirming the principle".

I need not enlarge very much on the history of the Cymru Fydd Movement, for Mr. William George has written a booklet on the subject, entitled *Cymru Fydd, Hanes y Mudiad Cenedlaethol Cyntaf*.[41] I have no need to repeat what he has to say, but merely to note the main facts, and to add a few facts which he omitted through lack of space, and some others which are outside the scope of his book. Mr. William George was right in emphasising the nationalism of Tom Ellis and Lloyd George, for the tendency of some Liberal historians has been to over-emphasise their Liberalism and to tone down their early nationalism. Mr. George also tried to trace the origins of Cymru Fydd, but discovered no definite source. There is, however, specific evidence on the beginnings of " Cymru Fydd " by a press correspondent in his report on a meeting in London. The report is entitled " Home Rule for Wales. A great meeting in London ":—

> At his side was the keen patriot, Mr. Thomas Ellis, M.P., in whose rooms, about two and a half years ago, the Cymru Fydd Movement was begun.[42]

If this evidence is true, the Cymru Fydd Movement originated in 1886, the year Tom Ellis went to Parliament. 1895 was the most important year for the Movement.

In *Y Faner*, February 2, 1895, appears a report of the formation of the Cymru Fydd National Federation, where it is stated that the South Wales Liberal Federation, the North Wales Liberal Federation, and the Cymru Fydd Federation, had within recent weeks appointed a joint committee of eighteen persons, who represented all parts of the country, to frame a constitution for the new National Federation. The constitution was designed on the basis of the existing constitutions of the two Liberal Federations, and that of Cymru Fydd, for the purpose of obtaining a constitution which would be acceptable by the three bodies, and under which every Welsh nationalist and every Liberal could work together whole-heartedly.[43] Mr. Alfred Thomas, M.P., D.A. Thomas, M.P., and Mr. J. Herbert Lewis, M.P., were appointed treasurers to the movement until the

---

41. i.e., Cymru Fydd. A history of the earliest national movement.
42. *Y Celt*, May 31, 1889.
43. *Baner ac Amserau Cymru*, Feb. 6, 1895.

meeting of the National Federation to appoint permanent officers. Early in January 1895, the South Wales Liberal Federation met in Cardiff and agreed unanimously on the following resolutions :—

    1. That it would be desirable to unite in one body the powers of the South Wales Federation, North Wales Federation and Cymru Fydd.

    2. To appoint and announce one committee of the three Federations to draw up a new constitution.

    3. That a General Conference of the three Federations should be held as soon as possible to accept and adopt the new constitution.[44]

A joint Committee was formed to draw up the constitution, and to fix the time and place of the Conference, but in a scantily attended meeting of the Southern Committee, it was decided to ' ignore everything, and to pay no more attention to the Constitution'.[45] It would appear that the Constitution which it was decided to ignore was that of the joint committee of the Cymru Fydd National Federation; although the South Wales Liberal Federation was represented on the joint-Committee; but it should be noted that it was a " scantily attended meeting of the South Wales Committee " which opposed. The Committee meeting was postponed for a week. " When the Committee met in a week's time, early in March, the two following resolutions were passed :—

    1st. The commitments of the January Conference should be carried out, and a meeting arranged at Aberystwyth with the other two Federations to adopt the new constitution, and to discuss the question of Disestablishment.

    2nd. The annual meeting of the South Wales Federation should be held in Aberystwyth at the same time to enable all members of the Federation to take part in these important matters.[46]

Was this a new Committee, or does it imply a change of opinion on the part of the original committee ? The account appears a little complicated, but it is evident that the working committee of the South Wales Liberal Federation was rent by a difference of opinion, and an undercurrent of dissension. " But last week," according to the *Faner*, " and that within a fortnight of the date appointed for the Conference and the annual meeting of the Federation, we learn that Mr. R. N. Hall, the Secretary, has announced

---

44. *Ibid*, April 10, 1895.
45. *Baner ac Amserau Cymru*, April 10, 1895.
46. *Ibid*.

that he fears that it will no longer be possible to hold the annual meeting of the Federation at Aberystwyth as arranged, and that it would be better to postpone that meeting, and hold it about Whitsuntide in some other town in South Wales."[47]

An account of " The Welsh National Conference", held in Aberystwyth, is given in *Y Faner*, April 20 and 24, 1895. After the various meetings had taken place, the Conference passed that the new Federation had been formed, namely " Cynghrair Cenedlaethol Cymru Fydd," or in English, " The Welsh National Federation". The South Wales Liberal Federation, The North Wales Liberal Federation, and the Cymru Fydd Federation no longer existed. The Conference was attended by members of South Wales branches of Cymru Fydd, of which there were forty, and by South Wales Liberals, but there was no official representation from the South Wales Liberal Federation. Two important points should be noted :—

(1) Cymru Fydd voted its own extinction as an independent body.
(2) The Welsh National Federation was not fully national for the South Wales Liberal Federation did not form part of it.

The *Faner* in its issue for April 24, 1895, was jubilant at the setting up of the National Federation, but in its next issue there appeared an article on " The Curse of Dissensions". An attempt was made to bring together the National Federation and the South Wales Liberal Federation, and it met with success. Each body sent seven representatives to a Conference at Llandrindod, where Mr. Brown proposed on behalf of the South Wales organisation that regional federations should be set up instead of a National Federation, and the Conference passed unanimously that four regions should be formed, namely

1. The Northern Region — Anglesey, Caernarvonshire, Denbighshire, Flintshire, and Merioneth.

2. The Mid-Wales Region —Montgomeryshire, Radnorshire, and Brecknockshire.

3. The South West Region — Cardiganshire, Pembrokeshire and Carmarthenshire.

4. The South-East Region —Glamorgan and Monmouthshire.

---

47. *Ibid.*

Branches should be set up also in the various counties, each Region should elect a committee, and these four committees should elect a National Committee. The original constitution had, therefore, to be re-cast. It is obvious that a small coterie in the South Wales Liberal Federation feared the authority of the Cymru Fydd National Federation and the motive behind Mr. Brown's proposal was to do away with that body. D. A. Thomas was chairman of the South Wales Liberal Federation and of the South Monmouthshire Committee, therefore the South-East Region, namely Glamorgan and Monmouthshire, the most thickly populated of the Regions, would be a tool in his hands.

All this manoeuvering led to confusion and disorder. The most important document relating to Cymru Fydd is the correspondence between Beriah Gwynfe Evans, and Llewelyn Williams on the one hand, and D. A. Thomas and others, which was published in the *South Wales Daily News* for 1895. It was a debate between the "Nationalists" and the "Cosmopolitans". According to the *Faner*, May 22, 1895, the South Wales Liberal Federation held a public meeting in Ferndale, which was addressed by Mr. Bryn Roberts, M.P., and D. A. Thomas, and "a number of gentlemen", with the purpose of opposing the National Federation, and advocating the continuation of the South Wales Federation. The names of the two main speakers are significant—Bryn Roberts represented the old Liberalism of 1868, and D. A. Thomas the English capitalist Liberalism of South Wales. Lloyd George, Herbert Lewis, and Llewelyn Williams addressed meetings in support of the National Federation. In January 1896, in a meeting of the South Wales Federation, the Nationalists came to final conflict with the Cosmopolitans. Mr. Robert Bird expressed the point of view of the Cardiff and Newport Cosmopolitans :—

> You shall see that there is a cosmopolitan population from Swansea to Newport who will never bow to the domination of Welsh ideas.[48]

In the above-mentioned correspondence, the Cosmopolitans raised the slogan "Wales for the Welsh" against the Nationalists, and it is a pity that the latter did not retort with "Wales for the Capitalists", but they were too Liberal for that. Within the Liberal Party there was a conflict of two Liberalisms : the rural Welsh Liberalism of Tom Ellis and Lloyd George, and the English Capitalist Liberalism of Lord Rhondda and Sir Alfred Mond. After flirting with Cymru Fydd, D. A. Thomas saw the red light ; he saw that Lloyd George's Welsh Nationalism was the worst enemy of the English capitalism of South Wales.

---

48. *Cymru Fydd*......,by William George, p. 42.

An attempt was made to revive Cymru Fydd. Thomas Gee's suggestion was that no further effort should be made to unite the South Wales Liberal Federation and the Cymru Fydd National Federation, but that each body should carry on its own work. Another suggestion was that the Cymru Fydd National Federation should fight it out, and continue to form its branches in every part of Wales, even in the Cosmopolitan districts. Llewelyn Williams's plan was to return to the original Cymru Fydd policy, and continue forming branches, but the difficulty was that the movement had moved its own extinction. The one thing done was the last thing that should have been done, and that was to ask the Members of Parliament to form a Federation, and thus was formed the National Welsh Liberal Federation; but this was merely a movement on paper, and a waste of paper at that.

Let us note briefly the main reasons for the failure of Cymru Fydd.

(1) *An Independent Welsh Party.*—The Liberals and the large majority of the Welsh Members rejected the counsel of Michael D. Jones, Emrys ap Iwan, and others, to form an Independent Welsh Party in Parliament. The weakness of the Liberal Party in Wales arose from the fact that it was part of the National Liberal Federation, and in this context 'National' meant English. After the opposition of D. A. Thomas and the others to Cymru Fydd, Llewelyn Williams saw that Welsh Nationalism would have no hope of success if Welsh Liberalism were tied to English Liberalism.

> If the Liberalism of England is incompatible with the Nationalism of Wales then we shall become Nonconformists in our politics as well as in our religion.[49] !

At the beginning of this chapter, it was seen that the English in Westminster had a majority of representatives over the three Celtic countries; this was no longer true as the Tories and Liberals were somewhat evenly balanced. The Irish Members, alone, could hold the balance. If each of the three countries had an independent party in the House, and a state of co-operation existed between the three, government would be impossible. They could change the Government every three months. Each of the three nations could obtain a measure of home rule as easily as winking. An agreement was reached between the Welsh Members under the chairmanship of Stuart Rendell; the Welsh were prepared to support Home Rule for Ireland on condition that the Irish Members would support Welsh Disestablishment of the Church. Parnell's adultery with Mrs. O'Shea brought the agreement to an end, and the Welsh Liberals turned for help towards the English and Scottish Liberals.

---

49. *Young Wales*, Vol. II, p. 31.

(II) *Nationalism.*—The leaders of Cymru Fydd had no definition of nationalism, nor of home rule. Llewelyn Williams described Welsh Nationalism as a vague and general thing, a spirit moving through the land. Their slogan was to " Codi'r hen wlad yn ei hôl,"[50] but they did not indicate clearly what they wished to restore. They had no concrete policies for agriculture and industry. According to the Liberals and the Agricultural Societies, Welsh farmers should have to pay reasonable rents, with interest on the money invested in the land, and obtain security of tenure. Dr. Pan Jones, however, who was a disciple of Henry George, (an economist of great influence in his day in America and in England, and also to an extent in Wales through his most remarkable disciple, Miss Helen Taylor) showed that this Liberal policy did not touch the problem of the ownership of the land. His policy was " The Land to the People," or the nationalisation of the land. Neither did the Cymru Fydd leaders indicate what kind of Home Rule they sought, but it can be gathered that their goal was a parish council of a Parliament.

(III). *Ignorance of Welsh History.*—Cymru Fydd had no future because the youth who had been taught in the schools of the 1870 Education Act, under the " Welsh Not", and with no attention to Welsh history, could not join it. Llewelyn Williams saw this clearly.

What avails it to form a National Party in Parliament if our Nationalism is sapped and undermined in every School in Wales?[51]

O. M. Edwards also declared that the weakness of Cymru Fydd was the ignorance of Welsh history among its members:

I feel that I have other work to do for Wales. Much of the misunderstanding between parties in Wales arises from the fact that no party understands the history of the Wales of the past. I would like to depict, as far as my limited ability allows, the olden days just as they were—and not from the angle of a Liberal or Tory, Methodist or Independent. What I would wish to do would be to explain the motives of the greatest heroes of our history,—but many of the readers of *Cymru Fydd* would expect me to sound the trumpet before Mr. Gladstone or Lord Salisbury.[52]

---

50. To raise the old country to its pristine glory.
51. *Young Wales*, Vol. I, p. 95.
52. *Cymru Fydd*, Vol. iii, p. 233.

And he took on himself the task of teaching the history and the literature of Wales to the Welsh people. *Cymru* appeared in August, 1891 ; *Cymru'r Plant* in January, 1892 ; *Wales*, a periodical to teach Welsh history and literature to English-speaking Welsh people, in 1894; *Y Llenor* in 1894; his book on Welsh history, and other books before the end of the century. His books were those of an educator and not of an historian, nor of a man of letters, for his purpose was to educate and not to create. Tom Ellis's nationalism came too soon to influence the Cymru Fydd Movement, and that of O. M. Edwards came too late.

(IV.) *Celtic Imperialism.*—The ' Celt ' became an important character in Welsh history and literature towards the end of the last century, and the beginning of the present. Renan and Matthew Arnold had brought Celtic literature to the fore, and had made it known to the English and on the continent of Europe. Matthew Arnold's influence is strong on the articles in *Cymru Fydd* and in *Young Wales* and on the writings of Tom Ellis. They looked on literature from the point of view of race, and that long before Hitler's day ; they held that the Celt was given to dreams and romance, was no statesman and politician, and that this was the reason for the political incompetance and helplessness of the Celtic countries: Britanny, Ireland and Wales. Tom Ellis and others did not agree, for was not Henry VIII, the greatest of statesmen, a Celt, and also Cromwell, who gave Britain a political commonwealth; and were not the leaders of the Methodist Revival also Celts ? The Celt was no narrow Welsh Nationalist, but a Welshman and a Briton, and that was one reason why a Celt like Tom Ellis took office in Parliament, and was followed in this course at a later date by Lloyd George, who was another Celt. In his tribute in Parliament to the Earl of Dwyfor, after his death, Mr. Churchill stated that the contribution made to Britain by this world-famous Celt was the greatest since that of the Tudors, and he spoke the truth. The Arch-Teuton conveyed England's thanks to the Celts.

The Cymru Fydd Movement and the nineteenth century drew to a close about the same time. Then victory went to Jac Glan-y-gors and not to Michael D. Jones, and that is the political tragedy of the nineteenth century in Wales.

D. GWENALLT JONES.

THE TWENTIETH CENTURY AND PLAID CYMRU.

MUCH of the difference in politics, as in other aspects of our life, between the 19th Century and 20th Century in Wales, became apparent with the turn of the century. The end of the 19th Century had seen the dissolution of Cymru Fydd; and the passing of Thomas Gee, Michael D. Jones, and T. E. Ellis marked the end of a period. Thomas Gee is the figure who perhaps typifies the best in the politics of the Wales of that century, and in nothing did he distinguish it more clearly from the nationalism of the early Twentieth Century than in his refusal of the knighthood which was offered him. In the Cymru Fydd movement he had "risen like a lion in his old age," but had failed to save Welsh radicalism from what has been called "the domination and damnation of the English Parties."

Two distinct strands can be discerned in Welsh politics at the end of the 19th Century; on the one hand the growth of Welsh Nationalism, and on the other the rise of a more conscious and aggressive British imperialism. The two competed for the loyalty of Welsh politicians, and the latter won the contest. As Gladstonian liberalism decayed the members of the younger generation of Liberal leaders were often as imperialist as the Tories. Few escaped the virus of imperialism. Even Lloyd George, whose campaign for peace by negotiation with the Boers, had been so courageous had never opposed the annexation of Boer Republics (Halévy, *Epilogue*, p. 176, Penguin Edition). The people of Wales were probably more anti-imperialist than their rulers, and it was on that ground, as well as a natural sympathy with small nations, that a large section of the community sympathised with the Boers.

In 1904 Lloyd George campaigned in Wales on a very different issue. His leadership of the revolt against the Balfour Education Act was the last time for him to appear in the role of a Welsh leader, if it would be a true description of him even then; for the inspiration of that campaign was almost solely Nonconformist, and there seems to have been little or no concern for the impact of the Act on Welsh education as such, either in its content or its organisation. Welsh Liberalism was, of course, very largely Welsh Nonconformity in political dress, and one of the major reasons for its decay in the course of the next two decades was the decline in the power of Nonconformity, hastened by the new tradition in its ministry of abjuring politics. But there was also a loss of power in the drive for self-government, which reflected the weakened fibre of Welsh Liberalism.

The Welsh National ideal waned as the new imperialism waxed, a deterioration which was to culminate in a Welsh Liberal conference crying down Llewelyn Williams's courageous protest against the infamies of the Black and Tans.

The change, however, went deeper than politics, and Arthur Price, one of the few nationalists of the Cymru Fydd movement who persisted in their nationalism through the next generation, who was not deceived by the apparently overwhelming majority gained by the Liberal party at the polls in 1906, described it at the time in this way :

> "Welsh Liberalism has grown cynical. The last General Election illustrated the power of Liberal organisation, and the unpopularity of the Establishment, and the squirearchy of Wales, but it called forth none of the patriotic enthusiasm of '86. A party of cynics has no place for one like Tom Ellis of the Cymru Fydd dawn."

Welsh Radicalism had for a time been inspired by the vision of Wales the nation marching forward to freedom and fulfilling its destiny in the family of nations. As the vision faded it succumbed to official English Liberalism, and was more than content with following the personal success of its leader, Lloyd George. The nationalist fire sank, only to flicker once or twice in the following generation, and now it is only the breath of the new Welsh Party which awakens an occasional gleam in its dying embers. But if its moral resources were exhausted it found compensation in the rise of its champion to Cabinet rank. "*He is our Mordecai*," declared Llewelyn Williams, "*who will procure for his people the right to rebuild the walls of Jerusalem.*" And the *Welsh Review* approved :

> "We believe that this is the proper attitude to take up. Let us make the most of the opportunity. Let us strengthen the hands of Mr. Lloyd George so that Wales may reap substantial benefits during his period of office. The entrance of Mr. Lloyd George into the Cabinet dealt a death-blow to the impossible dream of an Independent Party for Wales. There will be no more 'Parnells of Wales.' It was magnificent, but it was not politics. All Wales acclaims the new Cabinet Minister, and there is no one who accuses him of treachery or betrayal. He remains the Welsh leader and champion *whom the other Welsh members have been returned to support.*"

So that was what "politics" now meant for Welsh Liberalism, not the corporate struggle for a noble aim, but an obsequious subservience to the ascendancy of one man ; no policy for a nation however strong that man's passion for social justice. It is indeed a far cry from here to '86.

The advice was taken, but it was not Wales, but her leaders who reaped the "substantial benefits." For the parallel between the effect on Wales of Henry VII and Lloyd George can be taken farther than the seduction of the dominant class from their loyalty to Wales under the cloak of service to her ; it holds for the method adopted to confirm Welshmen in their new allegiance—a revolting system of rewards. The struggling nationalist movement was overwhelmed by an avalanche of offices and honours. Between this famous victory of 1906 and 1918 some three dozen Welsh M.P.'s received honours or appointments, and the policy, which was extended to a far wider field than the political, was apparently pursued with complete cynicism.

The Liberal victory in Wales in 1906 was held to "*reflect the rapid growth of a vehement spirit of nationalism in Wales.*" No doubt it did reflect the nationalism of the people of Wales ; it is the ordinary people of Wales who have been through the last four centuries the custodians of the Welsh tradition. It was not the people of Wales who failed, but their leaders. Had they leaders worthy of them, with strength enough to resist the fleshpots of the English Parties, they would by now have been led to national freedom. One of that generation was asked to point out the difference between Irish and Welsh nationalism. "*The leaders of Irish nationalism,*" he said, "*live a great deal of their time in gaol, and many of them die on the gallows. In Wales they live in comfort and die with a considerable amount of property to dispose of under their wills.*"

Not much was needed to keep the Welsh Parliamentary Party in its place. One searches in vain through these decades for a tribute of admiration to their selfless struggle for Wales, for although there were some very fine exceptions among them, they made no such struggle. The view expressed in April, 1906, by the Deputy Editor of the *Daily Chronicle* is typical of the opinion of patriotic Welshmen :—

> " The Welsh (Parliamentary) Party as such is a negligible factor in our national life. Where it ought to dominate it is utterly unregarded. It exerts no authority in Wales ; it wields no influence at Westminster. It has never evolved a programme or inspired a policy. Not once in its uneventful history has it heralded an advance in Welsh Politics."

When the new Parliament assembled Ellis Griffith proposed to the Parliamentary Party that its decisions should be binding upon its members, on all matters, but found only five to support him. Thus even when they were all drawn from one Party, there was no unity among them on Welsh questions. Such a " Party " does not even aspire to effectiveness. Marchant Williams said of them in his non-political quarterly *The Nationalist* (April, 1909—October, 1912) :—

> " Some of the Welsh M.P.'s are Specialists and look upon Welsh Nationalism as an ' extra subject'. In other words they paddle their own canoes, and they paddle well, but their canoes are very very small and of foreign make."

When we recall that in the 1906 election, Liberals, including six Lib.-Labs., were returned for every constituency in Wales except one in Merthyr Tydvil (which returned Keir Hardie), we can see how strong was the ground for calling Lloyd George " The Welsh Dictator." The Liberal Party had been the Nationalist Party of Wales. It built up that capital in the 19th century and has existed on it ever since. The long terms of office from 1906 are the period which saw it being squandered most prodigally. At once we see Lloyd George making the time-honoured appeal not to harass the Government, proclaiming at Caernarvon before the year was out that " *those who harass the Government when it was training its artillery on the House of Lords ought to be sent to the guardroom.*" No Government is without a substitute for this role of the House of Lords, and no Government has failed to find it an effective method of keeping its Welsh supporters quiescent.

By 1910 the place which had been won for Wales in British politics at the end of the 19th Century had been forfeited, and as the same representatives, more or less, were re-elected in that year, the tale is one of continued decay. It is true that there could still be disorderly scenes at public meetings on the Disestablishment of the Church and that the Temperance issue was still alive, but apart from this Welsh Liberal politics merely reflected what was happening in England.

Hence, when E. T. John introduced his Government of Wales Bill in March, 1914, he was able to find only a dozen M.P.'s to support him. The Bill was intended to further Federal Home Rule, but of course stood no chance of acceptance by the Government. It was, however, supported by thorough research, which proved to the satisfaction of the sponsors that under Home Rule the Welsh taxpayer would be in a more favourable position. For years the work for Home Rule is associated closely, if not exclusively, with the name of E. T. John, which will always be an honoured name in Welsh political history. Nevertheless he lost his seat in 1918 together with other good nationalists.

The Welsh cultural movement, as distinct from the political, went from strength to strength in this period. It was the heyday of *Y Beirniad, Cymru* and *Y Geninen,* of new life in poetry, prose, literary criticism and industrial research ; and this development was to prove far more fruitful than the sterile politics of the time. It is to this period that we owe the National Library, the National Museum, and the Welsh Department of Education, which was given through the influence of Lloyd George as a sop for the failure to secure a Council of Education for Wales.

In nothing had the Liberal party in Wales failed to prove itself a Welsh National party more than in its failure to sympathise actively with the efforts of the workers' movement for social justice, and were it not for the record of Lloyd George in social legislation, that failure would have brought about its nemesis sooner. It was extremely vulnerable to the accusation that it was not a Party representing the whole nation, but a class. Even in Caernarvonshire it showed no sympathy, far less active support, for the quarrymen in the Penrhyn strike, to give an instance.

The Labour movement advanced with the century, and the story contains some of the finest chapters in modern Welsh history. We are dealing now not with a movement in decay, but with the growth of a movement whose star was in the ascendant.

The Independent Labour Party was formed, after a generation of propaganda, in 1893. It did not immediately capture a large section of the people, and in Wales its advance was surprisingly slow. Although it could put up 28 candidates in the election of 1895, in 1900 the number throughout Britain was only 10, and there was no apparent growth of membership. Growth came at this period, not by slowly building up a Socialist party based on individual membership but by Trade Union affiliations. In 1899 the Trade Union Council had established the Labour Representation Committee to secure the return of Labour members of Parliament. It was this which became in 1906 the Labour Party, and its growth was greatly stimulated by the Taff Vale Judgment, which more than any other single factor, brought Trade Unions into politics.

We have seen that of the Welsh M.P.'s returned in 1906, Keir Hardie alone had stood independently for the I.L.P., although 29 I.L.P. members were returned in England and Scotland ; and in 1910 the position was unchanged except that the Lib-Labs. now belonged to the Labour Party. In that year 40 Labour members were returned in Britain, and of these, 39 won their seats in straight fights with the Tories through an understanding with the Liberals. From 1910 to 1914 the Labour party failed to win one of the many by-elections which it fought, and was frequently badly at the bottom of the poll, as in the case of Dr. J. H. Williams, in East Carmarthen. In January, 1912, the Labour candidate in Carmarthen Boroughs, which included Llanelly, could poll no more than 149 votes. The Party had made a particular effort to gain representation on the local authorities, but by 1907 had only 23 County Councillors in England, Wales and Scotland. I give these facts to show that the power of the Labour Party, despite the support of the Trade Unions, was not built up in a day.

At this time the Labour Party professed no concern for Wales ; it was absorbed almost exclusively in the economic problem, and had not seen that that problem was more capable of solution in a self-governing Wales than in a big imperialist country. Its press and pamphlets at the time have nothing to say of Wales, and her national problem is not discussed even in the Welsh-speaking section of the Party, as illustrated by David Thomas's *Y Werin a'i Theyrnas*. Significantly enough it did not succeed in maintaining a periodical of its own in Wales either in Welsh or English. Its first Welsh paper was indeed called *Y Gwladgarwr Cymreig* (The Welsh Patriot), but that did not save it from rapid extinction. The meetings of the I.L.P. were carried on in English even in the Welsh-speaking areas, unless there were present a Welsh leader who found it difficult to express himself in English, They were rare, for most of the leaders were immigrant Englishmen.

Keir Hardie was an exception, not only in being a Scotsman in Wales, but in his sympathy with national aspirations. He wrote in a message to the *Welsh Review* in 1906 :—

" My idea of what a national party should be is best exemplified in the workings of the Irish Parliamentary Party. . . . . A national party should, it seems to me, embody the thought, feelings, language, national life and aspirations of the people whose mouthpiece it is. It should gather up and focus the history and traditions of the country. In so far as I have succeeded in my life's work to create an I.L.P. it has been due to the fact that I have been inspired by an ideal, and have subordinated every interest, personal and political, to its realisation."

By 1910, however, Keir Hardie was asking, not for self-government for Wales, but, in a question in the House, " *whether it was the intention of the Government to create a separate administrative Department for Wales, with a Secretary of State responsible to Parliament.*" He received no answer, and his grandsons in the faith are still asking the same question. This measure was regarded as so innocuous that we find even the Conservative candidate for South Glamorgan saying in February, 1910 :—

" For years very little had been done for Wales, and if we are going to have its claims recognised the only possible way is through the appointment of a Minister."

This is the only reference I shall find it necessary to make to a Conservative, for the imperialism of the Conservative Party has been unrelieved by concern for the freedom of nations within the Empire, and has always viewed with fear and dislike the movement for Welsh freedom.

With the spread of industrialism the number of English and other immigrants increased. The flow reached its peak with the 1914—18 war, and many have since returned. In 1911, of the 2,420,921 population of Wales, 467,213 were born outside Wales

(388,238 in England). In that year there were 257,589 persons of Welsh birth in England, of whom 45 per cent had emigrated from the North and 55 per cent from the South. The majority of these immigrants came, of course, into the industrial areas of Glamorgan and Monmouth. They formed one of the major complications of Welsh politics for the rest of our period.

It was the time of the most rapid growth of trade unionism in Wales. The membership of the South Wales Miners Federation, for example, rose from 50,000 to 140,000 between 1898 and 1910. By 1914 South Wales had become " the industrial storm-centre of Great Britain," and it could be stated with truth that " *most of the movements which have agitated the minds of miners during recent years have either originated in South Wales, or have derived from South Wales their greatest support.*" This industrial unrest naturally concentrated the public mind in the populous areas on the class-struggle rather than the national struggle. There was at this time a heroism in the former which was lacking in the latter, and we can, as Welshmen, be proud of the leadership of our industrial workers in these years; but Wales the nation lost more than she gained from it. We had no Connolly in Wales to take the workers into the van of the national struggle, and to organise them as Welshmen in the economic struggle; no worker's leader who could say " The Socialists will never understand why I am here; they will all forget I am a Welshman."

Two other factors which weakened the Welshman's loyalty to Wales and lessened his power to think as a Welshman, were the educational system set up under the 1870 Act, whose harvest, together with that of 1889, was now being reaped; and secondly, the growth of the English press, which was supplanting the vernacular press throughout the country, and was, of course, uninterested in Wales. The cinema and wireless followed, and affected the springs of Welsh life even more profoundly.

Then came the War, whose first effect was to strengthen every influence which made for the destruction of Wales, and to weaken her traditional life. But its final outcome was not a weaker but a stronger national movement. This was not due to any political activity in the country as much as an elementary stirring of the national consciousness; but there can be no doubt that the influence of the Irish struggle was a potent factor.

The most active political movement in Wales in these years was the I.L.P., which had over a hundred branches in South Wales. It held some 20,000 meetings in the ten years from 1906 to 1916, and had distributed an immense amount of literature. For years it had held classes in a large number of branch rooms in economic political and other subjects, usually following the syllabuses of the Ruskin and Central Labour Colleges, but sometimes independent. For the most part the lecturers were men who had been to one of these two colleges; the Central Labour College, established in 1909 as the result of a split from Ruskin, was under the joint control of the S.W.M.F. and the N.U.R.

The policy of the I.L.P. was formulated in its branch rooms and since it attracted the ablest and most idealistic of the manual workers, and others such as teachers, and they were mainly young people, its influence far outweighed its numbers. The movement was far from being "respectable" even yet, but it was now clear that it had the future with it. A fact worth noting to illustrate the quality of the movement is that its funds were raised from personal subscriptions of members, and it was possible to say that "*no other political party is financed in as generous a manner by the individual members who compose it.*" The Syndicalists, of "The Miner's Next Step" fame, whose penchant was for industrial rather than political action, were a power at this time. Centred in the Rhondda, their permeation could win that area, and from there exercise a wide influence. Since the Rhondda was one-third of the South Wales coalfield, it could often carry the S.W.M.F., which in turn was the biggest constituent unit in the Miners Federation of Great Britain, whose policy on many important matters was thus decided in effect by a group in the Rhondda. This sense of power did much to stimulate the cosmopolitanism of the able trade union leader, whose ambition is still often unsatisfied until he gets "into the thick of things" as he regards it, in London.

The rising tide of Labour bore the Party within striking distance of power, but it had first to prove that it had the wider interests of the nation at heart. There is no doubt that its failure to take the national aspirations of Wales into account had been hitherto an obstacle to its growth, and had made it possible for "*Welsh-speaking Liberal Champions to win and hold their seats by playing upon the national feeling*" (*Welsh Outlook*, August, 1916). It therefore aspired to joining them in this activity, and so we read that "*latterly the Labour Party have become wiser political strategists*" in this respect (ibid).

It recruited many who were genuine nationalists, and was itself affected by the awakening national consciousness of the war years. In December, 1916, the South Wales Labour Federation was formed

> "to unify the political forces in Wales on a national basis and to give national expression and direction to the civic and social aspirations of the people of Wales *consistent with the wider outlook of the National* (sic) *Labour Party.*" (our italics).

The qualification shows how impossible it was for a Welshman to put Wales first if he joined the Party. A meeting of the organisations of both North and South Wales was "*to develop a Welsh National Labour Policy.*" This has not yet matured; there is still no indigenous Welsh Socialist policy. The Labour Party in Wales has taken its politics in their entirety from England, and when it has thought of Wales at all, has fitted it into the interstices of English policy; except of course at election time when each Labour Candidate is able to produce the Welsh policy which is most likely to attract his constituency.

By 1918 the position is clear. Though there were Labour leaders in South Wales who had no sympathy with Welsh national ideals, the majority of the Labour candidates in the constituencies were Home Rulers, according to *The Welsh Outlook*, and the general attitude of Welsh Labour was actually far more sympathetic than that of the adherents of the old Liberal Party. It was at this time that the leaders made the famous declarations on self-government, Ramsay Macdonald saying:

> "I have always been in favour of Home Rule for Scotland and Wales as well as Ireland. One of the most important measures of reconstruction after the war should be self-determination within this kingdom."

Arthur Henderson, who was more responsible than any other person for the building of the modern Labour Party, was an enthusiastic supporter of Self-Government. He understood the value of nationalism and could place his finger on its most serious weakness in Wales.

> "Nationalism," he wrote, "means the vigorous development of the material and moral resources of the whole people. It means a keener interest in the social, *political and industrial* problems which await solution. In my judgment, *the Welsh nationalist movement has not yet fully faced its political and economic responsibilities.* It is more concerned with the sentiment of nationality than with the practical concerns of Wales." (Our italics).

He was perfectly right, of course, but how he would have been derided by his fellow Labourites had he said that in the Wales of the Great Depression, and what taunts would have flown for his "economic nationalism." He advocated a Parliament for Wales because it would

> "encourage Welsh men and Welsh women to take an interest in their own affairs and to seek speedy and safe solutions of the *economic and social* problems that Wales, like every other community, must handle. Wales in this respect is a microcosm."

Imagine the difference in the history of Wales in the following years had his vision been shared by his fellow-socialists; what misery would have been avoided, what possibilities fulfilled! For he saw that—

> "it is hardly possible to conceive of an area in which a scheme of Parliamentary self-government on the federal basis could be established with better chances of success. All the problems which embarrass statesmen and challenge the imagination of reformers are to be seen in Wales reduced to manageable proportions. Given self-government Wales might establish itself as a modern utopia."

How different was to be the fate of a Wales which failed to struggle for self-government. It is significant that men such as Arthur Henderson and Keir Hardie who saw the vital importance of the nation in human society were Christians. As thought was secularised it became more cosmopolitan, losing its roots in the natural order.

Henderson stated categorically that the Labour Party, which was pledged to the widest measure of Home Rule for Ireland that could be devised, regarded the claims of Scotland and Wales as strictly analogous to those of Ireland. The policy was further stated in the Party's official statement of policy, *Labour and the New Social Order*, which declares that a form of federal Home Rule is an urgent necessity because of the incapacity of the Cabinet and the House of Commons to get through even its most urgently needed work. In June, 1918, the South Wales Labour Federation adopted a resolution in support of Home Rule and convened a special Labour Home Rule Conference in Cardiff in July. The Labour Party thus felt it had some right to aspire, in the words of its Welsh leaders, "*to become the true Nationalist Party in Wales.*"

These, however, were words spoken before an approaching election. When the election arrived, no serious attempt was made to make an issue of the future of Wales, because it would not " make a good stunt on the English political platform." It would have been a rather perilous issue in Wales itself for the candidate, because almost no educational work had been done in the constituencies. That is the most weighty part of the case against the Welsh Parliamentary representatives; that not only do they fail to make Welsh freedom the supreme issue at elections, not only are they inactive in the matter in the House of Commons, but that they do nothing to educate Wales in the urgent necessity of self-government. Many of them agree in principle with the justice of it and the need for it, but no one has heard of their campaigning assiduously through Wales to awaken the nation to make its demand united and unmistakeable, which they would assuredly do if their heart were really in the struggle. Until we have M.P.'s who are prepared to do this the Government, whatever its colour, will know that they can treat Welsh representatives very lightly.

Despite the failure of the Parliamentary candidates there was still a widespread demand for self-government in the country. A national conference at Llandrindod in June, 1919, attended by delegates from the large majority of local authorities, unanimously demanded full autonomy for Wales. The Welsh M.P.'s were asked to press the matter, but they preferred to retire behind that toothless old stalking-horse, the Secretary of State. Twice they tried, and twice Lloyd George advised them " to go for the big thing," advice which needless to say fell on deaf ears. The Secretary- ship was then rested between 1921 and 1937. One observes that it makes its appearance to Welsh M.P.'s at times of stress in their history, when Wales is frightening them by demanding action, as in 1891, 1919, 1937 and again recently. It indicates with remark- able accuracy the strength of national feeling in Wales, marking the occasions when it reaches the danger-point for her representatives.

The Liberals had, just before the 1918 election, suddenly remembered their concern for the cause which their Parliamentary representatives were doing their best to stifle, and Whitsuntide, 1918, saw them too holding a conference at Llandrindod to declare that they also favoured a comprehensive measure of autonomy for Wales, including a Welsh Parliament. There was some effort at the time to follow this up among the local authorities, but after the immediate post-war years they have made no further effort to implement the policy, apart from statements by their candidates when opposed by Nationalists. A Liberal organ which circulates in Merioneth, for example, had the effrontery to say during the 1945 election that if it was dominion status which Welshmen demanded the way to achieve it was through the Liberal Party! This from the Party which had for years held almost every seat in Wales, with a huge majority in Parliament and a Welshman as Prime Minister, but which utterly failed to bring Wales even within sight of the goal. It was capped, however, by the Labour Candidate in Mer- ioneth, who was not to be satisfied with so unambitious a policy. He was for independence!

In the meantime the Government had done its utmost for small nations from the Baltic to the Balkans, and before long it would be withdrawing the Black and Tans and making its Treaty with Ireland. But as *The Welsh Outlook* put it, though they " came before the world as the champions of freedom in Bohemia and Poland, to Wales they offer the policy of Edward I." They did have the grace, in October, 1919, to appoint a Speaker's Conference on Devolution, but since many of its members were openly opposed to the principle as applied to the nations of this island, not much fruit could be expected, and none was borne. One good effect which its proposals had, from their very feebleness, was the announcement by E. T. John, of his conversion from Federal Home Rule to Dominion Status.

Three elections followed in rapid succession in 1922, 1923 and 1924, and the concern shown in them for Welsh self-government lessened each time. Only a minority of the candidates, and those mainly of the Labour Party, referred to it, and despite the good work of the Union of Welsh Societies, which was active on behalf of Home Rule in these years, it was never a live issue. Two Labour members did table an amendment to the Address in 1922, to the King's Speech, deploring the omission of Welsh Home Rule.

The power of the Labour Party had grown rapidly during these years, and in 1922 it secured for the first time a majority of Welsh seats, L.G.'s alliance with the Tories having lost him much of his personal following in industrial Wales. The Party was in a position to seize its opportunity when it came, having prepared the way for years with intensive propaganda, and having built a powerful Party machine, and in particular in having efficiently organised Women's Labour Sections. They would soon be strong enough, unless challenged effectively, to ignore Wales altogether. The dissolution of the Liberals as a major English party was now in rapid process, and significantly the Tories in 1924 were stronger in Wales than at any time since 1874.

The Welsh Outlook, which had been so potent an influence under the editorship of Huws Davies, wrote of Wales in March, 1923 :—" Politically and *nationally we are at the ebb of our fortune* " ; and after the election of the autumn, 1924 :—" *At no election that we remember has so little attention been paid in Welsh constituencies to purely Welsh questions.*"

It was at this time, at the nadir of the fortunes of the national movement in its efforts to win Welsh freedom through one or other of the English Parties, that there appeared in the Welsh press correspondence and articles on the need of an independent Welsh Party. Those appearing in *Yr Herald Cymraeg* bore the name of H. R. Jones, a Deiniolen quarryman, who called a meeting in Caernarvon in September, 1924, for the purpose of considering the establishment of a new movement to further Welsh self-government. There he explained that what was needed, in his opinion, was a movement to continue the work begun by " Cymdeithas y Tair G " at the University College, Bangor. The new movement was formed and given the name of " Byddin Ymreolwyr Cymru " (Home-Rule Army of Wales). Three officers were elected, Gwallter Llyfnwy, President ; Ifan Alwyn Owen, Treasurer ; and H. R. Jones, Secretary. It was not many years before the three had died of the disease which has been so dread a scourge in Wales. The policy of the movement was to win self-government for Wales, without more minute definition, and to make the Welsh language compulsory in every Welsh court, school and institution. There were regular meetings, and the movement won the allegiance, among others, of the Rev. Lewis Valentine, Mr. Gwilym R. Jones, Miss Mai Roberts, Dr. R. Williams Parry, Llew Owain and Mr. Moses Gruffydd, and could claim some hundreds of supporters before the end of the year. Early in 1925, it formed itself into a political Party under the name " The Welsh National Party," and appointed a committee to act until the Pwllheli National Eisteddfod of that year.

About the same time new life was stirring in the South also. Just as the background influence in the North was a University College Society, so in the South a group who established at Aberystwyth University College a magazine called *Y Wawr* were responsible for a new political movement. *Y Wawr* was edited by W. Ambrose Bebb and Government intervention secured its suppression for nationalist and anti-war activities, in particular for an article by D. J. Williams. The immediate occasion of the formation of the new Welsh movement was the debate in *Y Geninen* between Mr. Ambrose Bebb and Prof. Morgan Watkin, and articles by the former, at the time a lecturer in Paris, in *Y Faner*. In January, 1924, Mr. Ambrose Bebb, Mr. G. J. Williams and Mr. Saunders Lewis, who became President, Treasurer and Secretary respectively, met at Penarth to form the movement. Its aim was to save Wales from her present state, and to make her a Welsh Wales; and to make the Welsh Language compulsory in Wales was to be its first direct objective. Wales alone was to be its sphere of work, and it was to work through the local authorities; should the movement fight Parliamentary elections no member would be free to take a seat in the London Parliament. As it had no organ of its own, it used the Breton periodical *Breiz Atao*, publishing in it articles in Welsh and securing for it a Welsh circulation. The first three recruits to the movement were Mr. D. J. Williams, who had in the meantime established the Labour Party in Pembrokeshire, Mr. Ben Bowen Thomas and the Rev. Fred Jones.

On his travels H. R. Jones contacted many of the Southern patriots such as Ambrose Bebb, Prosser Rhys and Dyfnallt, and he corresponded with Saunders Lewis. It was agreed that the two movements should unite on the basis of the policy suggested in a letter from Mr. Saunders Lewis, which was almost identical with the policy formulated in Penarth, with a heavy emphasis on the importance of working through the local authorities. They met together at the Pwllheli National Eisteddfod in August, 1925 (twenty-one years this week) and formed the Welsh Nationalist Party, with the Rev. Lewis Valentine as President, Mr. Moses Gruffydd, Treasurer, and H. R. Jones, Secretary.

The New Party made an immediate impression and caused considerable heart-searching among the Welsh elements of the English Parties. The Welsh press paid it a great deal of attention, but as yet it had no organ of its own to propagate its policy. This

was rectified when *Y Ddraig Goch* appeared in June, 1926, under
the editorship of Mr. Ambrose Bebb; it was subsequently shared
by Mr. Saunders Lewis and Dr. Iorwerth C. Peate, and then undertaken by Mr. Saunders Lewis, Professor J. E. Daniel and Mr. A. O. H.
Jarman in succession. In that number the article under Saunders
Lewis's name entitled " Nationalism and Capitalism," stated the
position of the party on the matter :

> " Let it be said immediately and definitely that capitalism is one of
> nationalism's greatest enemies. . . . . . It is the nation which creates
> capital . . . . . . Because it is the fruit of the energies of many working
> together and of the renunciation of many, it should be spread amongst
> the mass of members of the nation."

At the Pwllheli meeting it had been decided that an annual
summer school for the study and development of policy should be
established. The first such school was held at Machynlleth in
August, 1926. Of its 40 members, there are two here today, Miss
Kate Roberts and Mr. D. J. Williams, Llanbedr, who have been to
every intervening summer school. One of the most important
decisions made at that Conference was to engage a full-time organiser,
and the Executive appointed Mr. H. R. Jones to the post with an
office at Aberystwyth. In appealing for financial help *Y Ddraig
Goch* states :

> " The Welsh Nationalist Party is now a fact. We have succeeded
> in going beyond that condition in which men talk eternally of the
> yearnings of the Welshman, the nature of the Welshman, the ideals of
> the Welshman, and so on *ad nauseam* . . . the day of talk alone has
> passed."

Mr. Moses Gruffydd, the Treasurer, quite apart from his in-
valuable lead on agricultural and social questions, had his hands
full in trying to keep the movement sound financially, and in that
office performed the greatest possible service in these first critical
years.

From 1926 until 1939 the President of the Party was Mr. Saunders
Lewis, and upon his shoulders fell a great deal of the burden, not
only of the day to day leadership, but of defining the Party's policy
as it developed. From his pen we were to have, in *Y Ddraig Goch*
and *Y Faner* writing which, if it inevitably provoked profound
disagreement, compelled the attention of the enemies of the Welsh
Nationalist movement as well as its friends. Mr. Saunders Lewis's
generation of political writing, informed, consistent, passionate, will
surely be found to have been the greatest contribution ever made to
Welsh political thought. And among the great Welsh patriots of
two generations many will be found to call him the first.

From the beginning it had been a corner-stone of policy to aim
at representation for Wales on the League of Nations, and to put the
League, as the international authority, before Empire. The reverse
was the policy of English Government, Empire before League ;

but Wales is traditionally anti-imperialist, and nationalist Wales essentially so. Thus the Party aimed from the first at more than mere " devolution " ; it demanded for Wales the status of a free nation, but it was not until 1930 that its objective was definitely defined as Dominion Status, and Articles of Agreement prepared by a London Committee, including Arthur Price, E. T. John, Huws Davies and Mr. (now Judge) Alun Pugh.

The economic policy was, after the 1927 Summer School, soundly based on Co-operation and the division of property. Dr. D. J. Davies made important contributions towards its definition. He, above all, was the Executive's conscience in the matter of the capitalist exploitation of the Welsh miner, and its mentor with regard to the expansion and over-capitalisation of foreign combines in the coalfield. His emphasis on the importance of working in the industrial areas and of being prepared to use the medium of the English language more readily, has had its effect, and the removal of the Head Office to Cardiff indicates the seriousness with which the Party has taken to working vigorously in the anglicised industrial areas. In addition to this Dr. Davies has performed for this generation, in proving the economic benefits of self-government, the service which E. T. John did for his.

The end of the first five years saw the Party with the foundations securely laid of a policy for Wales, summed up in the phrase " Co-operative Welsh Democracy," which would give the movement strength and cohesion in the future. Its early optimism was sobered by the result of its first Parliamentary contest. Caernarvon County was the constituency chosen to fight in the 1929 General Election, and the Rev. Lewis Valentine was the candidate. The experience was indeed a baptism of fire. 609 votes were polled— " *Charge of the Light Brigade*," said the Rev. Fred Jones. But it was a historic occasion, the first time in Welsh history for a Parliamentary Election to be fought by an independent Welsh Party. It was, however, a harsh reminder that the battle of Wales was not to be won by a sudden rush, but that a long and arduous campaign would have to be carefully prepared, and the ground fought every foot of the way.

Hitherto the policy had been one of abstention from Parliament should Nationalists be elected. In the light of its reception in Caernarvonshire the policy was reviewed and changed at the 1930 Conference.

In June, 1930, H. R. Jones, the founder and first organiser of the Party, died. " *He was*," said Mr. Saunders Lewis, " *the purest of us.*" The party was more than fortunate to find Mr. J. E. Jones ready, at considerable personal sacrifice, to take up his work as secretary, and his vision, indefatigable industry and unwavering leadership have been one of the biggest formative influences in the subsequent growth of the movement, and have kept it on an even keel in more than one storm.

The period upon which we have now entered was one of the most difficult imaginable for a young party just beginning to find its feet. Wales found itself caught defenceless in the vortex of the worst economic blizzard in her history, a large section of her people uprooted and transferred elsewhere by the hundred thousand or left to rot in idleness and poverty. Her social and economic plight had been unhappy since the war, rent by industrial strife and drained by migration. Now her people were reduced to utter wretchedness. In the misery after the Napoleonic Wars she had the spirit to rebel; after the 1914/18 war she had not even that energy, and certainly not enough to insist upon taking into her own hands the responsibility for her own government. While the small nations of Northern Europe were rebuilding with the joy of creation their social fabric and resisting with success the effects of world depression, the once heroic people of Wales were sinking into an ever more craven dependence upon London Government. Their country becoming one of the worst slums of Europe, they were too demoralised even to dream of freedom. At least they had their doles now; things might be worse. In that spirit they accepted the abject failure of English Government in Wales, which had in its power a small, rich country of vast potentiality, and was making it into a desert.

The young Welsh Party preached its gospel of duty and responsibility towards Wales to deaf ears, and yet it persisted. It established an English monthly, called *The Welsh Nationalist*, and campaigned through the valleys of the South under the leadership of men like the late Morris Williams, Kitchener Davies and Wynne Samuel. It urged the local authorities to unite to make use of the power they already possessed to create new industries and provide a market for them. It established its " Thursday Dinner Club " for the unemployed men of some of the worst centres. It harried the Government and Welsh M.P.'s for more effective action in Wales, and presented plans for economic amelioration and reconstruction. There can be no doubt that this activity had its effect; the Party performed a service to the suffering people of Wales if only in existing as a threat to the status quo to which her representatives could refer in Government and official quarters while urging some concession. But more than that, it kept alive the consciousness and the rights of Wales the nation. Wales had not existed for many Socialists because it was not an economic problem to them; now it existed only as an economic problem, but not essentially different from any part of England

("Look at Jarrow" was always their retort, intended to prove that England was suffering as badly as Wales), and it was a desperate problem precisely because they had failed to look at it from any but the economic point of view.

In 1931 and 1935 the constituencies of Caernarvonshire and the Welsh University were fought by Prof. J. E. Daniel and Mr. Saunders Lewis with an increasing measure of success.

Then in 1936, Wales was rent by a tremendous controversy over the Government's proposal to establish in the Lleyn Peninsula an aerodrome and bombing school, as part of its re-armament programme. This vandalism if pursued unchecked in such Welsh areas as Lleyn might mortally injure the nation of Wales. Protests poured in from some 1,500 bodies and societies, mass meetings of protest were arranged and the Government was urged to receive a national deputation on the matter. It had done so in more than one case in England, but in Wales it refused. When all constitutional means were exhausted three Nationalist leaders burnt the bombing school and gave themselves up to the police. They were Mr. Saunders Lewis, Mr. D. J. Williams and the Rev. Lewis Valentine. At last an act of heroism had refreshed the sterility of the '30's. It revived the hearts of good Welshmen everywhere; only the self-seekers were angered and afraid. There was great enthusiasm when the jury at Caernarvon failed to agree to convict, and great indignation when the trial was removed to the Old Bailey to secure conviction, and a revival atmosphere welcomed the three back to Wales from Wormwood Scrubs in September, 1937.

Wales was not to be saved by enthusiasm alone, however; its determination had to be expressed in hard and constant work. This work proceeded with new vigour. But the clouds of war now overhung the world, and again distracted the minds of Welshmen from the work awaiting them in Wales. The Party had declared its opposition to all imperialist war, and demanded for Wales the right to decide for herself whether she should be belligerent or neutral. It led the fight against conscription which preceded the war, calling upon Welshmen to refuse, as Welshmen, to be conscripted into the English forces; and Wales saw a number of her sons standing in the dock as Welshmen against the power of England, and being sentenced to terms of imprisonment.

For four difficult years of war Prof. J. E. Daniel led the movement as President, and the service he rendered Wales in that period will not be forgotten. It was feared that the temerity of so unpopular a stand for the rights of Wales would involve the dissolution of the party. Far from being destroyed, however, it found itself at the end of the war, with Mr. Abi Williams now at the helm, in a far stronger position than at the beginning, strong enough in 1945 to fight ten seats in the Parliamentary election, and in 1946 to win 80 seats on the local authorities ; strong enough to increase its staff threefold and to open a new office in Cardiff.

Thus Wales finds herself after the last world war, whatever the perils of her situation, with this advantage over 1919, that she now has her own National Party, which has weathered the storms of 21 years and is now a political factor which will remain and increase in power. Did it not exist it would be necessary to create it, for the need today is more urgent that it has ever been. But an independent Welsh Party is a fact, and for that reason we face the future not only with resolve but with hope.

We have surveyed in these lectures nearly 2,000 years of the history of our nation. We have followed it in its greatness and its weakness through the crises of the centuries, which have seen the disappearance and oblivion of nations and languages, races and empires, and we ask ourselves now is there any reason for the astonishing persistence of this small community of ours ? Can there be a purpose inspiring its tenacious will to live ? And as Christian nationalists we can say that we believe that there is a value and a purpose in the life of Wales which is not to be lost, and that in fulfilling it, not only the life of her own people, but the life of the greater Society will be enriched.

We cannot fulfil this purpose, we cannot even survive as a nation, without national freedom, and so we will not rest until we have won for Wales the status of a free nation. That is the work for our generation. A generation ago it was the young men of the I.L.P. who were the driving force in Welsh politics ; two generations ago the young men of Welsh radicalism. In our generation let it be said that it is the youth of Plaid Cymru who are making the pace.

Let us move forward to our destiny together, the whole community of Wales, in our various callings, and our varied localities, whether our language be English or Welsh—we are one nation with a common past to rejoice in, a common present to labour in, and a common future towards which to strive.

GWYNFOR EVANS.

www.ingramcontent.com/pod-product-compliance
Lightning Source LLC
Chambersburg PA
CBHW021812220426
43662CB00006B/278